Rowan University

The
Domosh
Collection

A Gift

Keith & Shirley Campbell Library
Music Library at Wilson Hall
Frank H. Stewart Room & University Archives

THE CONFEDERATE REGULAR ARMY

By
Richard P. Weinert, Jr.

Foreword by
Archer Jones

WHITE MANE PUBLISHING COMPANY, INC.
1991

This White Mane Publishing Company, Inc. publication
was printed by
Beidel Printing House, Inc.
63 West Burd Street
Shippensburg, PA 17257

In respect to the scholarship contained herein, the acid-free paper used in this book meets the guidelines for permanence and durability of the Committee on Production Guidelines for Book Longevity of the Council on Library Resources.

For a complete list of available publications
please write
White Mane Publishing Company, Inc.
P.O. Box 152
Shippensburg, PA 17257

Library of Congress Cataloging-in-Publication Data

Weinert, Richard P.
    The Confederate Regular Army / by Richard P. Weinert, Jr. ;
foreword by Archer Jones.
        p.   cm.
    Includes bibliographical references and index.
    ISBN 0-942597-27-3 (lim. ed. : alk. paper) : $39.95
    1. Confederate States of America.   Army.   I. Title.
E545.W45   1991
973.7'13--dc20   91-2216
                                                                     CIP

3 3001 00971 8296

PRINTED IN THE UNITED STATES OF AMERICA

FOREWORD

This book not only does a superb job of illuminating an undeservedly obscure corner of Civil War history but shows that much of what little we know is wrong. Heretofore every authority has believed that the Confederacy's regular army existed only on paper, with the few officers who held regular commissions serving alongside and indistinguishably from the officers of the Provisional Army. Mr. Weinert not only shows that this is not true, but reveals its significant enlisted strength and faithfully narrates the far-flung and diverse campaigns of each of the regular units. In thus filling what all thought was a void with lively accounts of infantry, artillery, and cavalry units in many theatres with a variety of missions, he has entertainingly disabused us of our misconceptions.

In showing that many enlisted men in the Confederate Regular Army came from units of the United States Regular Army, the author explodes the myth, originated by Emory Upton, that all of these enlisted men remained loyal to the Union. Instead, these soldiers behaved in a manner one would have expected, had we given it any thought rather than followed the authority of Upton: many of those serving in units stationed in the South followed the Confederacy. And many deserted, as nineteenth century regulars were prone to do.

Part of the reason why Mr. Weinert has told a story that none believed existed is the thoroughness and perseverance of his research. Since beginning his work nearly thirty years ago, he has published three articles on the subject, including one in *Military Affairs* (now *Journal of Military History*) which won a Moncado Prize. Readers who pay attention to his footnotes will become aware of the breadth and depth of his research and notice an intriguing and sophisticated bit of detective work, one which helps explain why it took so long to understand the story. Typical of the difficulties encountered was his finding National Archives material on the Confederate States Army filed under South Carolina, someone long ago having carelessly made a mental transposition of the letters and put C.S. under S.C. Thus he found a treasure of source material misfiled under South Carolina.

But diligent and imaginative research did not lead him to write a dreary administrative history. On the contrary, by telling the story of all of the Regular Army's units he has given us an interesting and lively story which embraces almost every aspect of the war and is sure to tell even the most erudite buffs some things they never knew. Thus readability reinforces scholarly merit of this fine little book and helps commend it to a broad spectrum of readers.

Archer Jones
Richmond, Va

PREFACE

The history of the Civil War is studded with the stories of outstanding units. The most famous have had their deeds recorded in memoirs, official and semi-official histories, and scholarly works over the last hundred and twenty-five years. Most Civil War organizations, however, have not achieved such fame. A few, unfortunately, rather have been described at best inaccurately.

And then there are the few units of the Confederate regular army. What little has been said about these units is almost completely wrong. As if to add insult to injury, the Confederate War Department appears to have forgotten the existence of its own regular units for much of the war. Even the United States War Department, after the Confederate archives fell into its hands, for some reason consistently denied they ever existed.[1]

Several years ago I stumbled across records of one of these units in the National Archives. Intrigued by something that I had never heard of, further research began to reveal what the Confederate Regular Army was, what units and men composed it, and what they did during the war. A clear picture emerged regarding the Confederate government's attempts to organize for war, what actually happened, and the struggle of the regular units formed to fit into the volunteer army. The stories of the individual units provide a seldom considered view of small formations during the war. Though the Confederate regular army had no significant impact on the course of the war, the author hopes that this account will correct previous published errors, add

---

[1] The result historically can be seen in James M. McPherson, *Battle Cry of Freedom: The Civil War Era* (New York and Oxford: Oxford University Press, 1988), p. 328. McPherson says "The South, by contrast, had no regular army."

knowledge about some of the organizational problems of the Confederacy, and finally give long overdo recognition to the war time service of the officers and men who composed the Confederate regular army.

As always, many people and institutions helped to make this book possible. Especial thanks for reading the manuscript and for their comments go to Dr. John K. Mahon of the University of Florida, Dr. Warren Hassler of Pennsylvania State University, Dr. Archer Jones of Richmond, Dr. Jay Luvaas of the U.S. Army War College, and Col. Jerry V. Witt.

The staffs of the National Archives, U.S. Army Military History Research Institute, Mississippi Department of Archives and History, Museum of the Confederacy, Louisiana State Library, Hill Memorial Library of Louisiana State University, Louisiana Army and Air National Guard Headquarters at Jackson Barracks, the Tulane University Library, Museum of the City of Mobile, the University of Alabama Library, Alabama Department of Archives and History, and the Casemate Museum at Fort Monroe all contributed to the research. For their support of my early research on the Confederate regular army, thanks are also due to the late Dr. Victor Gondos of the National Archives, Dr. Arthur Ekirch and Dr. Dorothy Gondos of American University, and Ralph Donnelly. Earl Dashiell prepared the maps.

Richard P. Weinert, Jr.
Hampton, Va.

TABLE OF CONTENTS

Chapter I

THE CONFEDERACY
PREPARES FOR WAR

A new nation has to create all the many governmental and administrative agencies which are taken for granted in a long-established sovereign state. For a new government which is created by revolution the first and most important agency of sovereignty is an army. Any army can and will do for fighting the government's war of independence, but the new administration must create a regular standing army if it is to maintain at least an appearance of being a permanent government. The creation of a regular army in the midst of a revolution presents peculiar problems of its own. When a nation has ample time and reasonable security, such as the United States had following the close of the Revolutionary War, it can experiment, modify, revise, and even for a time abolish its army.

Thanks to the intricacies of the international relations at the time, the United States had easily gained recognition of its independence from many of the leading states of the world and eventually concluded an alliance with France which made the success of its revolution possible. No such favorable international climate greeted the Confederacy. There was plenty of sympathy from abroad, but also a wariness of recognizing a government which might not be able to maintain its independence.

An internal psychological problem also hampered the leaders of the Confederacy. They had been accustomed to a smoothly functioning government and believed that they were taking an action in withdrawing from the Union which was recognized by the United States Constitution. Their legalistic minds jumped to the conclusion that the transition would be smooth and peaceful and a government much like the one they had left would be quickly and easily created.

A state of war did exist in fact at the beginning of 1861 even if no overt hostilities had taken place. Recognizing this, it was natural for the Confederate government to see to the formation of an army soon after the establishment of a civil structure. And since the Southern leadership assumed that all would be as it was before, it was natural that a regular standing army should be one of the first military provisions. The politicians realized that a large volunteer force was immediately necessary, but the military would be built upon the regular establishment as much as possible.

The Confederacy modeled its army, as all its other governmental creations, after that of the United States. Because of the nature of the formation of the Confederacy there were reasonable expectations that at least a part of the old army could be taken over virtually intact to form the nucleus of the new regular army.

The United States had from the very beginning carried over the British distaste for a standing army, somewhat reinforced by its own experiences prior to the Revolutionary War. As a result, the regular army of the United States had never been adequate to perform the functions dictated by a vast and wild frontier, let alone fight a major war against a well organized enemy. The United States Army at the end of 1860 consisted of ten regiments of infantry, four regiments of artillery, two regiments of dragoons, two regiments of cavalry, a regiment of mounted riflemen, and the requisite staff departments. If all of the companies had been recruited to their full authorized strength the army would have numbered 18,318 officers and men to protect a population of about 31,400,000. The actual number of men in service on December 31, 1860, however, was only 16,367.[1] This small army was scattered from the San Juan Islands in Puget Sound to Fort Taylor in Key West and from Fort Preble, Maine, to Fort Mojave, California. Of the 198 companies composing the army, 183 were stationed west of the Mississippi River and only five were stationed in the coastal fortifications in the South.[2]

---

[1] *War of the Rebellion: A Compilation of the Official Records of the Union and Confederate Armies* (Washington: Government Printing Office, 1880-1901) 130 vols. (hereafter cited as *OR*), Series III, Vol. I, p. 22; *Army Register, 1861* (Washington: The Adjutant General's Office, 1861).

[2] Bvt. Maj. Gen. Emory Upton, *The Military Policy of the United States* (Washington: Government Printing Office, 1912), p. 225.

What they lacked in numbers, the officers of the United States Army in part made up for in quality. For the most part graduates of the United States Military Academy, they had received long practical experience in countless Indian wars and in the Mexican War. Slow promotion and the limitations imposed by the size of the army had forced many of its best officers back into civil life and most of the colonels and generals were antiquated. But the company officers on the whole were to prove their outstanding military abilities in the coming conflict.

The enlisted men presented something of an engima. The United States regular was looked down upon as a mercenary and the military life held few inducements for the average American. As a result, half to two-thirds of the regular enlisted personnel at this period were foreign born, with many only newly arrived in the United States.[3] Of the native born soldiers, a good percentage came from the dregs of society. These men were not citizen soldiers, they were professionals with a goodly portion having served several enlistments.[4]

Of the officers, about one-fourth joined the Confederacy, although many Southern officers chose to remain loyal. It cannot be denied that the Confederacy inherited many of the best regular officers, but not nearly as high a percentage as usually is assumed. The enlisted men, for many reason, for the most part remained loyal. That this fact has been overemphasized will be discussed later when events in Texas are more closely analyzed. But scattered for the most part far from civilization and with few if any state attachments, the enlisted men had little opportunity or incentive to go over to the Confederacy.

The United States realized that if it intended to raise an army large enough to suppress the rebellion, it would once more have to fall back on the citizen soldier. To counter this, the Confederacy at first also looked to its own citizen soldiers. Basic of these were the multitudinous, and often ephemeral, militias of the various states. Of probably more use in the long run were the state armies which were formed as each Southern state declared its independence. From these "state regulars" came some of the finest regiments of the Confederate Army.

To properly understand the place of the Confederate regular army in the history of the Civil War, it is necessary to examine the way the Con-

---

[3] Ella Lonn, *Foreigners in the Union Army and Navy* (Baton Rouge: Louisiana State University Press, 1952), pp. 80-89.

[4] For an excellent discussion of the enlisted men of the pre-war army, see Edward M. Coffman, *The Old Army, a Portrait of the American Army in Peacetime, 1784-1898* (New York and Oxford: Oxford University Press, 1986), pp. 137-211.

**SAMUEL COOPER
GENERAL, C.S.A.**
*Museum of the Confederacy.
Courtesy of a private collection.*

federacy raised its forces to fight the United States. In order to appreciate the problems confronting the Confederate government, it is also necessary to examine in some detail the regular army structure envisioned at the start of the war. The following chapters will show how far short of this goal the Confederacy fell.

It might be well here to clarify the difference between the Confederate regular army and the much more numerous "state regulars." According to General Samuel Cooper, the Adjutant and Inspector General of the Confederacy, "There are no *regular* troops authorized by acts of Congress other than those duly enlisted for the *regular army* of the Confederacy. What are called *state 'regulars'*, created under acts of State Legislatures, form no part of the regular army of the Confederate States, and when in the service of the Confederacy, can only be regarded as part of the Provisional Army, like all other volunteers in the service of the Confederacy..."[5]

The Provisional Army of the Confederate States was formed under authority of an act of Congress passed February 28, 1861. The legislation authorized the President to accept into Confederate service any units in state service for a period of twelve months.[6] Under an act of March 6, 1861, a call for 100,000 volunteers was made and the acceptance of the various state militias was authorized.[7] Although not technically part of the Provisional Army, these troops in practice came to form a part of it.

Also on March 6, 1861, Congress passed "An Act for the establishment and organization of the Army of the Confederate States of America."

---

[5] Cooper to Secretary of War, May 31, 1862, endorsement on letter of Maj. John D. Munford, 1st Virginia Infantry Battalion, Compiled Military Service Records (hereafter cited as *CMSR*), War Department Collection of Confederate Records, Record Group 109, National Archives (hereafter cites as *NA*).

[6] *Statutes at Large of the Provisional Government of the Confederate States of America* (Richmond: R. M. Smith, Printer to Congress, 1864), Chapter XXII, Section 3 (hereafter cited as *Statutes*).

[7] *Ibid.*, Chapter XXVI, Section 1.

SECRETARY OF WAR
LEROY POPE WALKER
Courtesy of the Casemate Museum.

This act established the regular army. To help in preparing this act, Colonel William J. Hardee had been called from Georgia to Montgomery, Alabama. Hardee, a distinguished senior cavalry officer in the old army, was probably best known for his *Light Infantry Tactics*, which became the standard drill manual of the Civil War. From February 27 to March 21, Hardee worked closely with Secretary of War Leroy Pope Walker and General Pierre G. T. Beauregard in writing the army bill.[8]

The major staff departments, with the exception of the Corps of Engineers, had previously been authorized on February 26, 1861, but no provision had been made at that time for line troops. The Act of March 6, 1861, provided for a Corps of Engineers, Corps of Artillery, six regiments of infantry, one regiment of cavalry, and additional governance of the other staff departments. The Act of March 6 was deliberately conservative, forming a smaller military establishment than that of the United States, but adhering to the principles of military organization familiar to its Confederate authors.

The highest rank provided for in the regular army was that of brigadier general. The law authorized four brigadiers and an aide-de-camp for each, selected from the lieutenants of the line. The Act of March 14, 1861, increased the number of brigadier generals to five.[9]

Promotion was strictly by seniority and was to be made regimentally or by corps in the staff departments, Artillery, and Engineers. The exception seems to have been the appointment of brigadier generals which "shall be made by selection from the Army."[10]

The Act of March 6, 1861, adopted the Articles of War and Army

---

[8] Nathaniel Cheairs Hughes, Jr., *General William J. Hardee: Old Reliable* (Baton Rouge, Louisiana State University Press, 1965), pp. 70-71.

[9] *Ibid.*, Section 8 and Chapter XLI, Section 2.

[10] *Ibid.*, Chapter XXIV, Section 11, and Chapter XLI, Section 2.

Regulations of the United States Army by simply changing "United States" to "Confederate States." The Confederate *Army Regulations, 1861* was in effect the same as the *Army Regulations, 1857* of the United States Army. The 1862 edition contained a few additional changes. Articles 61 and 62 of the Articles of War were the only ones completely revised. Article 61 dealt with brevets and is not important since the Confederacy never awarded any brevet commissions. Article 62 dealt with seniority for command and will be discussed later. All military laws of the United States which did not conflict with the Confederate Constitution or laws were also continued in force.

The Adjutant and Inspector General's Department was originally authorized an Adjutant and Inspector General with the rank of colonel, four assistant adjutants general with the rank of major, and four assistant adjutants general with the rank of captain. This was changed by an act of Congress of March 14, 1861, so that the Adjutant and Inspector General was a brigadier general, a fifth brigadier being added to the total in service, and there would be two assistant adjutants general with the rank of lieutenant colonel, two assistant adjutants general with the rank of major, and four assistant adjutants general with the rank of captain. The change was in part the result of the fact that Colonel Samuel Cooper, The Adjutant General of the United States Army at the beginning of 1861, had been appointed the senior brigadier general in the Confederate Army. Another act added an assistant adjutant general with the rank of colonel on October 8, 1862.[11]

The Quartermaster General's Department, as provided for in the Act of February 26, 1861, was to consist of a Quartermaster General with the rank of colonel, six quartermasters with the rank of major, and as many assistant quartermasters as might be needed. The assistant quartermasters were to be detailed from the lieutenants of the line. On May 16, 1861, an act was passed which added one assistant quartermaster general with the rank of lieutenant colonel and two quartermasters with the rank of major. In addition to their other duties, all quartermaster officers were authorized to act as paymasters.[12]

The Commissary General's Department was originally to consist of a Commissary General with the rank of colonel, four commissaries with the rank of captain, and as many assistant commissaries as needed to be detailed from the lieutenants of the line. This was altered on March 14, 1861, so that there would be one commissary with the rank of lieutenant colonel, one commissary with the rank of major, and only three commissaries with the

---

[11] *Ibid.*, Chapter XVII, Section 11; Chapter XLI, Section 1; and Chapter XXXV.

[12] *Ibid.*, Chapter XVII, Section 3, and Chapter XLI, Section 3. The provisions regarding paymasters were objected to by Secretary Walker in his report of April 27, 1861, but no separate Pay Department was established. *OR*, Series IV, Vol. I, p. 250.

rank of captain. On May 16, 1861, one assistant commissary with the rank of major and one assistant commissary with the rank of captain were added.[13]

The Medical Department was to consist of a Surgeon General with the rank of colonel, four surgeons with the rank of major and six assistant surgeons with the rank of captain. As many additional assistant surgeons could be employed on a contract basis as needed. On May 16, 1861, six surgeons and fourteen assistant surgeons were added to the regular establishment. On the same date, the Medical Department was authorized to enlist as many hospital stewards as necessary with the pay and allowances of sergeant major.[14]

It was soon realized that the small regular army would need to expand to fulfill its function. On May 16, 1861, Congress passed "An Act to increase the military establishment of the Army of the Confederate States and to amend the 'Act for the establishment of the Army of the Confederate States of America.'" General Cooper appeared to have been the main inspiration for this revision. The changes effected in the four staff departments have been noted above. The Act of March 14, 1861, appears to have been an ill-timed effort by Congress at penny-pinching and the Act of May 16 served in part to rectify this.

The line was expanded by the addition of a regiment of cavalry and two regiments of infantry. Although no attempt was ever made to organize these units, their authorization was important because most of the additional officers were appointed.[15]

This act rectified a situation which had nearly brought chaos to the new Confederate Army. Under the 62d Article of War adopted March 6, 1861, command devolved upon the senior officer present according to commission without regard to whether it was an Army, Navy, Marine Corps, or militia commission. Since no regular officer held higher rank than brigadier general, command of large numbers of troops was falling to inexperienced officers with state volunteer or militia commissions. The Act of May 16 abolished to the rank of brigadier general and changed it to full general so that regular general officers outranked anyone they might serve with. Those officers who had been appointed brigadier generals were automatically promoted to full general.[16]

The brigadier generals appointed in order of seniority under the March 6 act were Samuel Cooper, Robert E. Lee, and Joseph E. Johnston. Cooper

---

[13] *Ibid.*, Chapter XVII, Section 4, and Chapter XLI, Section 4. This department was usually called the Subsistence Department.

[14] *Ibid.*, Chapter XVII, Section 5; Chapter XX, Section 7; and Chapter XLI, Section 7.

[15] *Ibid.*, Chapter XX, Section 1.

[16] *Ibid.*, Section 2.

GENERAL ROBERT E. LEE
Courtesy of the Casemate Museum.

probably became the senior officer because Lee and Johnston did not actually resign from the United States Army until after Virginia seceded in April. Pierre G. T. Beauregard was nominated as brigadier general, but the rank was changed to full general before the Senate acted. On August 31, 1861, Albert Sidney Johnston was appointed to the remaining vacancy, but was placed second in seniority to Cooper. The relative rank reflected the seniority of these officers in the United States Army, but caused resentment on the part of Joseph E. Johnston which rankled throughout the war. Johnston had at the time of his resignation held the staff rank of brigadier general as Quartermaster General of the United States Army while the others with the exception of Beauregard had been colonels. Cooper had been The Adjutant General and Lee and Albert Sidney Johnston commanded cavalry regiments while Beauregard was a brevet major of Engineers. Following the death of Albert Sidney Johnston at Shiloh on April 6, 1862, Braxton Bragg was appointed general in the regular army with seniority as of that date. Bragg had not held a regular commission and was serving as a major general in the Provisional Army. Subsequently, Edmund Kirby Smith, who was a lieutenant colonel of regular cavalry, was appointed a full general in the Provisional Army and John B. Hood, who was a regular cavalry captain, received a temporary appointment of full general in the Provisional Army.[17]

The Corps of Engineers was increased by the Act of May 16, 1861, by the addition of one lieutenant colonel and five captains. Six military store keepers with the rank of first lieutenant were also added.[18]

This act also recognized the need for training junior officers and, until a military academy could be established, cadets were to be attached to line companies as supernumerary officers for training. Although a naval academy was eventually established, no military academy came into being. Many of these cadets were to receive commissions as second lieutenants in the regular army or to be commissioned in the Provisional Army before the end of the war. The system was basically the one used by the United States Army in the years immediately prior to the establishment of the military academy at West Point.[19]

One of the most important provisions of this act was the granting of temporary rank, corresponding to their duties, to regular officers serving in staff positions with volunteer troops.[20] A bounty of $10 was provided for

---

[17] Regular Army Register, Chap. I, Vol. 88, RG 109, NA. Douglas Southall Freeman, *R. E. Lee, a Biography* (New York and London: Charles Scribner's Sons, 1934), Vol. I, pp. 501, 559. Ezra J. Warner, *Generals in Gray* (Baton Rouge: Louisiana State University Press, 1959), pp. xv, xxiv. Warner incorrectly says that the six generals were the only officers to receive regular commissions.

[18] *Statutes*, Chapter XX, Section 3.

[19] *Ibid.*, Section 8, and Regular Army Register, Chap. I, Vol. 88, RG 109, NA.

[20] *Statutes*, Chapter XX, Section 9.

each recruit enlisted in the Army of the Confederate States. This does not seem to have been made retroactive and so had little if any effect on recruiting for the regulars. In fact, the records are not clear that any regular recruits ever received this bounty.

Congress also made various other minor modifications. The most important of these was an act passed on May 21, 1861, which allowed the President to give regular officers temporary rank to command volunteer troops. Most of the regular officers served as general and field grade officers under this act. Congress amended this act on December 31, 1861, to include officers serving with the Adjutant and Inspector General's Department, Chief of Engineers, and Chief of Ordnance.[21]

The regular army authorized by these laws would have been composed of slightly over 15,000 officers and men. A tabular breakdown of its organization is in Appendix B.

---

[21] *Ibid.*, Chapter XXX.

Chapter II

ORGANIZING THE
CONFEDERATE REGULARS

H aving established the legal framework of the regular army, the Confederate War Department next turned to the much more difficult task of recruiting and organizing the men.

The first step in organizing the new regular army was the appointment of the officers. Nearly 25 percent of the officers of the United States Army joined the Confederacy and many officers who had left the army earlier also offered their services.[1] In order to avoid arguments over seniority, the Act of March 14, 1861, provided that all United States officers who resigned and joined the Confederacy within six months should be commissioned as of the same date and take seniority by their original United States commissions.

There were many more positions available than former United States officers. In the early months appointments were given to civilians with no prior military experience, but none of these were to higher rank than captain. The military cadets provided for did not enter service until late 1861 and were never enough in numbers to fill the large number of vacancies for

---

[1] Francis B. Heitman, *Historical Register and Dictionary of the United States Army* (Washington: Government Printing Office, 1903), 2 vols.

lieutenants. Most of the officers having formal military training came from the United States Military Academy. These ranged from seasoned officers who graduated near the top of their class, such as Robert E. Lee, to cadets still in school who were to prove their ability, such as Oliver Semmes.

An idea of the background of the regular officers may be gained by examining a few of the officers who will appear later in these pages. Colonel Earl Van Dorn was a West Pointer; Lieutenants Alexander Haskell and Edward Ingraham had been officers in the United States Army, but not West Pointers; Lieutenant James Baltzell was a graduate of the Virginia Military Institute; and Lieutenant John Bradley was appointed from civil life, but may have had enlisted service under the United States. Lieutenant Edward Powell had served for twenty years as a noncommissioned officer in the United States Army; Lieutenant John H. Denys was promoted from the Confederate ranks and may have had previous United States enlisted service. Lieutenant Oliver Semmes and Lieutenant John A. A. West were cadets at West Point at the beginning of the war. Several graduates of the Citadel also held regular commissions.

With most of the officers appointed, the next problem of the Confederate War Department was to recruit the enlisted men for the regular units. The most successful recruiting efforts, which took place in Texas, the Mississippi Valley, and Baltimore, will be discussed in detail in the following chapters. Recruiting in the eastern states of the Confederacy for some reason was not successful. The companies ultimately formed in Charleston were recruited for the most part in Baltimore, which was not even in the Confederate States.

To receive the expected influx of recruits, the War Department set up a series of recruiting depots at which the men would be received, equipped, organized, and trained. The depot at Baton Rouge Barracks, described in a succeeding chapter, was the largest. Other posts designated as recruiting depots were San Antonio Barracks, Texas; Mount Vernon Arsenal, Alabama; Augusta Arsenal, Georgia; Castle Pinckney, South Carolina; Fort Johnston, North Carolina; and Bellona Arsenal, Virginia.

On April 13, 1861, Captain Thomas H. Taylor had been placed in charge of recruiting operations in the Mississippi Valley and 1st Lieutenant Robert C. Hill was transferred from that duty to North Carolina. Colonel Theophilus H. Holmes was named superintendent of recruiting in North Carolina with the hope that he could form his 2d Infantry Regiment.[2]

Captain Dorsey W. Pender, who had closed down the recruiting station

[2] Cooper to Hill, May 3, 1861, and Cooper to Holmes, April 22, 1861, Letters Sent, A&IGO, Chap. I, Vol. 35, pp. 91 and 56, RG 109, NA.

in Baltimore when hostilities made it impossible to forward recruits, was also ordered to report to Holmes. Other regular officers assigned to Holmes on recruiting duty were Major William H. C. Whiting, Corps of Engineers, and Captain Frederick L. Childs and 1st Lieutenant Joseph P. Jones, Corps of Artillery. At the suggestion of Colonel Holmes, the recruiting depot was transferred from Fayetteville to Fort Johnston in Smithville at the mouth of the Cape Fear River.[3]

The War Department was quick to move recruiters for the regulars into Virginia when that state seceded. Captain John Scott was ordered to start recruiting in Richmond on April 22, 1861. Captain G. W. Carr was assigned to command the depot at Bellona Arsenal near Richmond and Captain Edward J. Harvie was put on recruiting service in Norfolk.[4] Even before the recruiting officers arrived in Virginia, eager citizens were reporting large numbers of men ready to enlist. On April 23, 1861, Scott was directed to establish a temporary rendezvous at Alexandria, just across the Potomac River from Washington, D.C. But the problems faced by all regular recruiters quickly materialized in Virginia. On April 26, Carr was ordered to Harpers Ferry to muster volunteers into the service and on April 27 both Scott and Harvie were ordered to muster volunteers at Richmond. While they were thus engaged in forming the Provisional Army, recruiting for the regular army was allowed to lag.[5]

A somewhat ludicrous situation also snarled recruiting in Richmond. On the assumption that Bellona Arsenal had been Federal property, the Confederate War Department designated it as the recruiting depot for Virginia and Captain Carr and his recruits occupied the premises thirteen miles up the James River from Richmond. On May 24, 1861, Dr. Junius L. Archer irately informed the War Department that Bellona Arsenal was his property and he would appreciate the removal of the troops. Being a little patriotic, however, he offered to sell the property to the Confederacy. Somewhat sheepishly, General Cooper ordered Carr on May 28 to immediately withdraw and informed Archer that if they ever really needed the Arsenal the government would consider his offer. Actually, Bellona Arsenal went on to produce heavy ordnance for the Confederacy for the remainder of the war.[6]

---

[3] Cooper to Holmes, May 2, 1861, Letters Sent, A&IGO, Chapter I, Vol. 35, p. 87. Recruiting officers in North Carolina were assigned per Special Order No. 40, May 1, 1861; No. 41, May 2, 1861; No. 42, May 3, 1861, No. 44, May 6, 1861; and No. 46, May 10, 1861, A&IGO; RG 109, NA.

[4] Cooper to Scott, telegrams of April 20, 22, and 27, 1861; Cooper to Harvie, April 22, 1861, Letters Sent, A&IGO, Chap. I, Vol. 35, pp. 54, 57-59, 72. For further instructions regarding recruiting in Virginia, see Cooper to Scott, May 15, 1861, Letters Sent, A&IGO, Chap. I, Vol. 35, p. 117, RG 109, NA.

[5] Cooper to George C. Wederbum, April 23, 1861; Cooper to Scott, April 23 and May 4, 1861; Cooper to Scott, telegrams of April 26 and 27, 1861, Letters Sent, A&IGO, Chap. I, Vol. 35, pp. 61-62, 93, 71-72; RG 109, NA.

[6] Cooper to Carr and Cooper to Archer, May 28, 1861, Letters Sent, A&IGO, Chap. I, Vol. 35, pp. 151-152, RG 109, NA.

A problem of another sort faced the Confederate government at Mount Vernon Arsenal. Here recruiting for the regulars ran into direct conflict with recruiting for the Provisional Army and the volunteers. Besides being the regular army depot for the area, Mount Vernon Arsenal was also serving as the rendezvous for the majority of Alabama troops. As a result of correspondence with the Adjutant General of Alabama, General Cooper issued specific instructions regarding recruiting to Captain James L. White, commanding Mount Vernon Arsenal, on April 8, 1861. White was directed to send sufficient men to fill the contingent at Fort Morgan near Mobile at the entrance to Mobile Bay. Then the recruits enlisted up to February 28 were to be mustered into the Provisional Army. Those recruits enlisted after that date were to be organized into volunteer companies. When all this was done, White was authorized to begin recruiting for the regulars. Obviously not many men would be left.

The War Department soon realized that there were not enough regular officers available to take care of all the recruiting. It fell back on the expedient of hiring civilian recruiting agents. Apparently the first was R. B. Kyle of Gadsden, Alabama, who was authorized on April 27 to begin recruiting in northeast Alabama. It was necessary, however, for the actual enlistments to be signed by regular officers. For this purpose Lieutenants W. de B. Hooper and S. F. Rice were ordered to Gadsden. The situation faced by the regular army was expressed by Cooper to Kyle when he wrote, "...As these officers are both quite young and entirely inexperienced in regard to the important duties of the recruiting service, I beg to impress you with the necessity of your giving close examination of the moral and physical qualities of the men who are enlisted. ..." These recruits were supposed to be sent to the recruiting depot at Mount Vernon Arsenal.[7]

It was not until May 3 that the regular recruiting depot was established at Mount Vernon Arsenal. On that date, First Lieutenant John Mullins was assigned to command the depot. Although Cooper optimistically estimated that there would be 200 recruits, it appears that the handful actually obtained was recruited by R. B. Kyle and his green lieutenants.[8] At least one recruit, Private Simeon McDonald, was discharged while the depot was still in operation. On June 15, 1861, Lieutenant Mullins reported the breaking up the depot.[9]

---

[7] Cooper to White, April 8, 1861, and Cooper to Kyle, April 27 and 29, 1861, Letters Sent, A&IGO, Chap. I, Vol. 35, pp. 27-28, 75, 77-78, RG 109, NA.

[8] Cooper to Mullins, May 11, 1861, Letters Sent, A&IGO, Chapter I, Vol. 35, p. 106, RG 109, NA; and OR, Series IV, Vol. I, p. 209.

[9] Order No. 4, Recruiting Depot, Mount Vernon Arsenal, Ala., June 12, 1861, "Unfileable File" for Simeon McDonald; Special Order No. 129, A&IGO, August 20, 1861; Mullins to Cooper, June 15, 1861, Register of Letters Received, A&IGO, Chapter I, Vol. 45, p. 142; RG 109, NA.

Apparently all of the regular recruits remaining at Mount Vernon Arsenal were transferred to Fort Morgan. Colonel William J. Hardee had been commissioned to command the 1st Infantry Regiment and assigned to duty in Mobile. Hardee apparently wanted five companies of Georgia troops that he had organized before receiving his Confederate commission, but these were not offered by Governor Joseph E. Brown of Georgia.[10] Whatever the original intention, the Mount Vernon Arsenal recruits were formed into an Ordnance Detachment under the command of First Lieutenant Charles D. Anderson, Corps of Artillery. This detachment at Fort Morgan consisted of two officers and nine enlisted men. It was mustered separately, but for administrative purposes was attached to the 2d Alabama Infantry, which formed part of the garrison of Fort Morgan. Anderson was the post ordnance officer and his detachment handled the routine ordnance duties of the fort. On November 9, 1861, Anderson became major of the 20th Alabama Infantry and command of the detachment devolved on Second Lieutenant Alfred M. O'Neal.

In April 1862, the 2d Alabama Infantry was broken up at the expiration of its term of service. Many of the enlisted men reenlisted in the 1st Confederate Infantry Battalion, a Provisional Army unit, to which O'Neal was assigned. Ultimately, he was promoted to captain in the Provisional Army. Although the Ordnance Detachment was never actually part of the 2d Alabama Infantry, it too was broken up at this time. One of the men joined the 1st Confederate Infantry Battalion and the others were transferred to Company A, 1st Alabama Artillery Battalion. Two men eventually deserted, one was discharged, four were captured when the forts guarding Mobile fell, one was paroled with the 5th Company, Washington (Louisiana) Artillery at the end of the war, and one was last reported in a hospital. One of the men captured died while a prisoner of war. The composition of the detachment is interesting for two reasons. All the men were recruited in Gadsden and all were native born Southerners.[11]

Recruiting in Georgia centered upon Augusta Arsenal. Captain Robert G. Cole was named to superintend the recruiting and branch stations were opened at Macon and Milledgeville. The recruits at Charleston were originally to have been transferred to Augusta Arsenal, but recruiting in Georgia was

---

[10] Hughes, *Hardee*, p. 71; *OR*, Series I, Vol. LII, Part 2, p. 24. When the second regular cavalry regiment was authorized, Hardee was transferred to the cavalry branch.

[11] Muster Rolls of a Detachment of Recruits of the Army of the Confederate States, August 31 and October 31, 1861, filed with 2d Alabama Infantry Muster Rolls; *CMSR* 2d Alabama Infantry and 1st Alabama Artillery Battalion. Anderson had been appointed a first lieutenant, his former rank in the United States Army, when he joined the Confederates and was then promoted to captain when the appointments were actually sent to the Senate. He had not been notified of his promotion. The same thing also happened to Mullins. On June 13, 1862, Anderson wrote the War Department about his rank and was finally informed of his promotion. *CMSR*, Col. C. D. Anderson, 21st Alabama Infantry, RG 109, NA.

so poor that it was decided to reverse the process and send the Georgia recruits to Charleston.[12]

Anderson's Ordnance Detachment in Alabama was composed of regular army line recruits. In Savannah, another Ordnance Detachment was formed under the same authority as the Baton Rouge Arsenal Ordnance Detachment, which will be discussed in a later chapter. The Savannah detachment consisted of one officer, a sergeant, and three privates. The enlisted men had originally enlisted in the 1st (Olmstead's) Georgia Infantry, a state regular unit, in February 1861. Five men from this regiment were permitted to be discharged on July 9, 1861, to enlist in the Ordnance Department, but only four of them are subsequently picked up on the detachment muster roll.[13]

Ordnance Sergeant Harvey Lewis and Private John Parker were captured at Fort Pulaski, Georgia on April 11, 1862, but were exchanged in August and rejoined the detachment. The detachment served at the Savannah Ordnance Depot until Union troops under Major General William T. Sherman captured the city on December 21, 1864. Unlike the Baton Rouge Arsenal Ordnance Detachment, which was engaged in the manufacture of ordnance supplies, the Savannah unit was only concerned with repairs and distribution. The detachment's first commander was Captain Richard M. Cuyler, Corps of Artillery, a former lieutenant in the United States Navy. He was succeeded in command of the detachment and as ordnance officer of the District of Georgia by First Lieutenant Alexander T. Cunningham, Provisional Army. There is no record of the detachment after the fall of Savannah.[14]

The difficulties encountered by the recruiting officers in Richmond have already been recounted. The regular infantry detachment which had been recruited by Captain Scott was transferred back to the city from Bellona Arsenal under the command of Captain Carr on May 28, 1861. On June 6, First Lieutenant David H. Todd, the brother of Mrs. Mary Todd Lincoln, was ordered to Richmond.[15] He took over command of the detachment and on July 1 was placed under the command of Brigadier General John

---

[12] Cooper to Cole, May 3 and 13 and June 12, 1861, Letters Sent, A&IGO, Chapter I, Vol. 35, pp. 90, 111, 180. For assignment of officers to recruiting duty, see Special Orders No. 40, May 1, 1861, and No. 41, May 2, 1861, A&IGO, RG 109, NA.

[13] Muster Rolls, Cunningham's Confederate Ordnance Detachment; Special Order No. 73, District of Georgia, July 9, 1861; RG 109, NA.

[14] *CMSR*, Cunningham's Confederate Ordnance Detachment, RG 109, NA. Thomas H. S. Hamersly, *Complete General Navy Register of the United States of America from 1776 to 1887* (New York: T. H. S. Hamersly, 1888), p. 187.

[15] Special Order No. 65, A&IGO, June 6, 1861, RG 109, NA. Todd had been on recruiting duty in Wilmington, N.C.

H. Winder, the provost marshal of Richmond. Todd served as prison commander until his transfer to the 1st Kentucky Infantry in September. In 1862, he was promoted to captain in the 21st (Patton's) Louisiana Infantry. Todd was accidently killed on August 5, 1862, at the Battle of Baton Rouge, perhaps shot by his own men.[16]

Todd was succeeded in command of the regular detachment in July 1861 by 2d Lieutenant William B. Ochiltree, Jr. The regulars were mainly assigned to guarding prisoners of war and provost duties. In addition to these duties, men from the detachment were also detailed as orderlies and couriers in the various War Department bureaus. The detachment was broken up in November 1861. Ochiltree spent the remainder of the war as a quartermaster first lieutenant in Texas. Of the twenty-six recruits who formed the detachment, one died of an accidental gunshot wound, four deserted, nineteen were transferred to Company E, 1st Virginia Regular Infantry Battalion, one was transferred to Company C, 18th Virginia Heavy Artillery Battalion, and there is no final records for one.[17] The 1st Virginia Regular Infantry Battalion was a state regular unit and acted for most of the war as the provost guard of the Army of Northern Virginia. The battalion participated in all the major campaigns in Virginia. During the war six of the Confederate regulars were captured, one was wounded and retired, four were discharged, there is no final record for four, five deserted, and two died while prisoners. The one man in the 18th Virginia Heavy Artillery Battalion was captured at Farmville, Virginia, on April 6, 1865, and paroled along with two men of the 1st Virginia Regular Infantry Battalion at the end of the war.

No other units of the Confederate regular army were organized except for those described in the following chapters. A few individual members of the Confederate regular army served in the Ordnance and Medical Departments or as couriers and orderlies at various headquarters. The number of such regulars could not have been large and it is impractical to try and identify their service.

Besides the regular recruiting efforts, several offers were also received to accept volunteer campanies into the regular army. The recruiting of Jules V. Gallimard of New Orleans probably falls in this category and will be considered later. On March 25, 1861, the Governor of Mississippi forwarded to the War Department the offer of a company which had been formed. The War Department replied on April 5 that under existing laws there was no

---

[16] Regular Army Register, Chapter I, Vol. 88, RG 109, NA. William C. Davis, *The Orphan Brigade, The Kentucky Confederates Who Couldn't Go Home* (Baton Rouge: Louisiana State University Press, 1980), pp. 116-117, says it was Capt. *Alexander* Todd, a brother of Mrs. Lincoln, who was killed at Baton Rouge.

[17] Special Order No. 85, A&IGO, July 1, 1861; *CMSR*, Ochiltree's Detachment of Confederate Regular Recruits; R. H. Chilton to Scott, June 21, 1861, Letters Sent, A&IGO, Chapter I, Vol. 35, p. 208; RG 109, NA.

authority to accept fully organized companies into the regular army. The War Department would agree that if all the men individually enlisted in the regulars to assign them all if possible to the same company. The officers could not be accepted unless there were vacancies available and they passed the prescribed examination for civilian appointees. This last point seems to have finished the matter.[18]

A combination of the hastily written laws, inexperienced officers, and makeshift organization of the recruiting service led to problems at all the recruiting stations. The foremost problem was probably the matter of bounty. The recruits enlisted in Baltimore apparently were promised some kind of bounty, but found on their arrival in Charleston that this was illegal. The local and state bounties being offered for volunteers made it difficult, if not impossible, to obtain men for the regular army. Until the regular army bounty law was finally passed, the War Department fell back on the not too happy expedient of offering a two dollar bonus to anyone who brought in a recruit. This, of course, did the recruit no good, but it apparently did induce some men who enlisted to go out and find other men for the regulars in order to get the bonus.[19]

The physical examination of the recruits was another major problem. The doctors of the Medical Department were so few in number and so badly needed with the newly forming armies, that none could be spared for the recuiting service. As a result, it was necessary to hire private doctors in the areas where recruiting was being done.[20]

Clothing presented a problem in the early days. Uniforms were not available despite the fact that they were minutely described in Army Regulations. A temporary uniform was devised and each regular recruit arriving at a depot was to receive a forage cap, a blue shirt as a blouse or sack coat, gray overalls, and the necessary underclothing. Despite the fact that recruits began to gather in March 1861, even this makeshift clothing issue does not appear to have been available until the end of April. Since many of the men were literally swept off the streets, it was often necessary for the recruiting officers to spend money not only for their food and transportation, but also for enough clothing to get them to the depots.[21]

---

[18] J. H. Hooper to Hon. W. P. Harris, April 5, 1861, Letters Sent, Secretary of War, Chapter IX, Vol. 1, pp. 138-139, RG 109, NA.

[19] Cooper to Frazer, April 19, 1861; Cooper to Taylor, May 2 and 7, 1861; Cooper to McCall, May 4, 1861; Cooper to Kyle, May 10, 1861; Cooper to Scott, May 12, 1861; and Cooper to Hooper, May 18, 1861; Letters Sent, A&IGO, Chapter I, Vol. 35, pp. 50, 88, 94-95, 99, 104, 110, and 127, RG 109, NA.

[20] Cooper to Grayson, May 15, 1861; Cooper to Scott, May 15, 1861; and Cooper to 2d Lt. J. T. Mason Barnes, May 15, 1861; Letters Sent, A&IGO, Chapter I, Vol. 35, pp. 116-118, RG 109, NA.

[21] Cooper to Taylor, April 22, 1861; Cooper to Scott, April 22, 1861; and Cooper to Harvie, April 22, 1861; Letters Sent, A&IGO, Chapter I, Vol. 35, pp. 55, 57-59, RG 109, NA.

The organization of the regular army quickly became caught up in the problems facing the War Department in forming the much larger Provisional Army. On April 1, 1861, Secretary of War Walker, in a communication addressed to Attorney General Judah P. Benjamin, called attention to the complications in the several acts of Congress providing for a regular army, a Provisional Army, and a volunteer service, and in making provision for the support of these three distinct military organizations. Walker stated that it was not altogether clear to his mind out of which appropriations the troops then in service should be paid. He called attention to the several laws bearing on the subject and requested an official opinion in regard to them. Benjamin replied that from the confused

JUDAH P. BENJAMIN
Courtesy of the Casemate Museum.

way the troops were mustered into service it was impossible to clearly tell the difference between the volunteers and the Provisional Army. As Congress had appropriated enough money to run the regular army as envisaged in the various acts, but nowhere near that many men had been recruited for the regulars, he advised that the War Department use the regular army appropriation to defer the Provisional Army expenses until Congress could untangle the mess.[22]

By June 1861, recruiting for the regular army began to fall off badly. Enlistments in the regulars can be found as late as 1862, but the vast majority of the men who served with the regulars had enlisted by the end of June. Because of the pressing need of the Provisional Army for officers, and probably as a result of a decision to use regular army funds for the Provisional Army, it was decided to close down the recruiting stations and transfer the recruiting officers to duty in the field. On May 24, 1861, the stations at Pikesville, Montgomery, Florence, Frankford, and Gadsden in Alabama and at Vicksburg, Mississippi, were closed. On June 6, 1861, the stations at Mount

---

[22] *OR*, Series IV, Vol. I, p. 202. Rembert W. Patrick (ed.), *Opinions of the Confederate Attorney General, 1861-1865* (Buffalo: Denis & Co., Inc., 1950), pp. 6-8.

Vernon Arsenal and Mobile, Nashville, Wilmington, Macon, Milledgeville, and Augusta also were closed.[23]

It is impossible to tell exactly how many men enlisted in the regular army. From the muster rolls and returns that have survived, it appears that there were approximately 800 enlisted men who served at one time or another in the regular army. Added to these were approximately 850 officers and cadets who received regular army appointments. The total of a little more than 1,600 officers and men is a far cry from the 15,000 envisaged by Congress and the War Department.

The atmosphere surrounding the formation of the regular army and the ensuing frustration is well illustrated by the following comments of Thomas Cooper De Leon:

> The skeleton of the regular army had just been articulated by Congress, but the bare bones would soon have swelled to more than Falstaffian proportions, had one in every twenty of the ardent aspirants been applied as matter muscle. The first "gazette" was watched for with straining eyes, and naturally would follow aching hearts; for disappointment here first sowed the dragon's teeth that were to spring into armed opponents of the unappreciative power.[24]

John B. Jones had just embarked on his career as the "Rebel War Clerk" and also was struck by the potential dangers arising from the appointments in the regular army. "May 20th (1861) — ...The applications now give the greatest trouble; and the disappointed class give rise to many vexations."[25]

Without a doubt the most important regulars in the Confederate Army were the officers in the various War Department bureaus at Richmond. Under the Act of February 26, 1861, the Adjutant and Inspector General's Department, Medical Department, Commissary Department, and Quartermaster Department were created as previously discussed. With the modifications necessary to handle the large volunteer army, this organization was continued throughout the war. The senior positions in these staff departments were occupied by regular officers serving with their regular army rank with few exceptions. Because there were few opportunities for Provisional Army promotions in these staff positions, almost all the regular army promotions

---

[23] Cooper to Capt. Theodore O'Hara, May 24, 1861, Letters Sent, A&IGO, Chap. I, Vol. 35, p. 142; Special Orders No. 58, May 24, 1861, and No. 65, June 6, 1861, A&IGO. The fall in the number of enlistments may be seen in the following entries in the Register of Letters Received, A&IGO, for which no letters have been found: Taylor, Nashville, Tenn., May 30, 1861; 2d Lt. W. B. Ochiltree, Fayetteville, N.C., June 5, 10, and 15, 1861; Capt. F. L. Childs, Wilmington, N.C., June 12 and 17, 1861; 1st Lt. C. W. Phifer, New Orleans, La., June 25, 1861; and Capt. W. S. Walker, Memphis, Tenn., July 6, 1861; Chap. I, Vol. 45, pp. 224, 164, 162, 175, and 262, RG 109, NA.

[24] Thomas Cooper De Leon, *Four Years in Rebel Capitals* (Mobile: The Gossip Printing Co., 1890), p. 26.

[25] John B. Jones, *A Rebel War Clerk's Diary* (Philadelphia: J. B. Lippincott Co., 1866), Vol. I, p. 38.

during the war were received by officers in the staff departments. The other major exception to the promotion policy was in regard to cadets promoted to second lieutenants which will be discussed later.[26]

A discussion of the activities of the regulars in the staff departments would involve the entire military policy of the Confederacy, a subject much too broad for this study. Only a few observations relating directly to the regular army will be made here.

There was no consistency in regard to the rank of the senior officers of the staff departments. Samuel Cooper became the Adjutant and Inspector General, the equivalent of the position he had held in the United States Army, but received the regular army rank of full general. The senior officers of the other staff departments held the regular army rank of colonel. Of these, Jeremy F. Gilmer was eventually promoted to the Provisional Army rank of major general. Gilmer saw much service in the field and the administration of the Engineer Department often devolved on Colonel Alfred L. Rives, a Provisional Army officer.[27]

The Commissary and Quartermaster Departments were subject to the most criticism during the war. The attempt of President Davis to promote Colonel Lucius B. Northrop, the Commissary General, to brigadier general in the Provisional Army was rejected by the Senate. The case of Abraham E. Myers, the Quartermaster General, is an even more interesting example of the way in which regular and provisional rank could be used in juggling staff positions. Myers had been appointed Quartermaster General with the regular army rank of colonel. On March 20, 1863, Congress passed an act authorizing the Quartermaster General to hold the Provisional Army rank of brigadier general. Since Myers had fallen into disfavor he was not nominated for promotion and instead Brigadier General Alexander R. Lawton was assigned to the position and the appointment ratified by the Senate. Lawton was a West Pointer, but had resigned from the United States Army in 1841 and was not commissioned in the Confederate regular army. The appointment of Lawton in fact legislated the unfortunate Myers right out of the army. The Attorney General held that the act creating the Quartermaster General a brigadier general in the Provisional Army had in effect abolished the position of Quartermaster Department colonel in the regular army and left Myers without any rank.[28]

---

[26] Regular Army Register, Chap. I, Vol. 88, RG 109, NA.

[27] Warner, *Generals in Gray*, p. 105. The organization and administration of the Engineer Department, with adequate coverage of the regular army, is contained in James L. Nichols, *Confederate Engineers* (Tuscaloosa: Confederate Publishing Co., Inc., 1957).

[28] Warner, *Generals in Gray*, pp. 175-176, 225-226; Thomas Robson Hay, "Lucius Northrop: Commissary General of the Confederacy," *Civil War History*, VI (May 1963), pp. 5-23; *Opinions of the Confederate Attorney General*, pp. 428-437.

The Ordnance Bureau, the other major staff department of the War Department, is unique in that it never legally existed. On April 8, 1861, Major Josiah Gorgas, Corps of Artillery, was appointed Chief of the Bureau of Ordnance. When the final regular ranks were submitted to the Senate he was commissioned lieutenant colonel in the Corps of Artillery. Subsequently Gorgas received promotions to colonel and brigadier general in the Provisional Army. The Ordnance Bureau ultimately became one of the most important staff departments, but it was never legally constituted. Ordnance duties had been assigned under the Act of March 6, 1861, to the Corps of Artillery and this is probably the origin of the Ordnance Bureau. Benjamin Huger, the colonel of the Corps of Artillery, had been promoted to major general in the Provisional Army. When he proved to be an incompetent line commander he was named as Inspector of Artillery and Ordnance in 1862, a position actually similar to the one he would have held in the regular army.[29]

The War Department actions in regard to the promotion of cadets were almost as badly bungled as the handling of the expiration of enlistment terms. President Davis at the beginning of the war made it a rule not to commission any officer in the regular army who had not reached the age of twenty-one. The ones most vitally affected by this decision were the former cadets at West Point who joined the Confederacy. Men who had reached their majority were commissioned while those who still were minors, even though they might have had a higher standing at West Point, were made cadets. By the time the latter were of age, the War Department had forgotten about the matter. After protest from the men involved they usually were promoted to second lieutenants in the regular army. Again no consistent policy was shown. Some were promoted simply for coming of age if their Provisional Army service had been satisfactory, others had to take the regular cadet promotion examination before a board of officers.[30]

The importance of the regular army officer corps in the Provisional Army is hard to judge. Many of the regular officers ultimately received line commissions in the Provisional Army and served with distinction. Because the regular officers did not hold positions under the individual states probably a majority of them ended up as staff officers with the field armies of the Provisional Army. Perhaps the best indication of the importance of the regular army officer corps can be gained by examining the general officers of the Confederate Army.

---

[29] Special Order No. 17, A&IGO, April 8, 1861, RG 109, NA. Warner, *Generals in Gray,* pp. 112, 143-144; *OR,* Series IV, Vol. III, pp. 943-944; *Army Regulations, 1862,* Article 44.

[30] The problems in regard to promotion policies are illustrated in the *CMSR,* Staff File, RG 109, NA, of the following officers: W. E. Stoney, W. Q. Hullihen, and G. A. Thornton.

There were eventually commissioned in the Confederate Army, under a variety of acts, 8 generals, 17 lieutenant generals, 72 major generals, and 328 brigadier generals. Of these, all 8 generals, 7 lieutenant generals, 28 major generals, and 64 brigadier generals were regulars. Even more impressive is a comparison of the number of regular officers of field grade who served as generals: all 8 infantry colonels, 8 of 9 infantry lieutenant colonels, 6 of 8 infantry majors, both of the cavalry colonels, both of the cavalry lieutenant colonels, both of the cavalry majors, the artillery colonel, both of the artillery lieutenant colonels, and 6 of the 11 artillery majors. The various staff departments, especially the Corps of Engineers, also provided several generals.

While most of the company grade regular officers served in higher company or field grades in the Provisional Army, there were a few instances of spectacular rises in rank. The largest increase was 2d Lieutenant Pierce M. B. Young, Corps of Artillery, who became a major general; 2d Lieutenant Frank C. Armstrong, was a brigadier general; and 1st Lieutenant Fitzhugh Lee was a major general. Three of the regular army first lieutenants who became general officers in the Confederate Army — Fitzhugh Lee, Joseph Wheeler, and Thomas L. Rosser — were also to become general officers in the United States Army during the Spanish-American War.[31]

Despite confusion, conflicting laws, poor recruiting, and an early loss of most of the regular army appropriation to the Provisional Army, the Confederacy did manage to establish a regular army. The press of events and the necessity of quickly creating a vast volunteer force prevented the regular army from completing its organization. Nevertheless, the regular officers played an important role during the war. In the following pages we will look at the activities of the few regular units to actually take the field during the war.

---

[31] This comparison was drawn from material in Warner, *Generals in Gray,* and the Regular Army Register, Chap. I, Vol. 88, RG 109, NA. The totals follow Warner and include several officers, such as Northrop, who were never actually confirmed by the Senate as generals.

Chapter III

THE CONFEDERATE REGULAR CAVALRY

S pring was in the air on the desolate plains of west Texas. In remote frontier posts the scattered companies of the United States Army prepared for another season of compaigning against the Commanches and the Lipans. The commander of the Department of Texas as 1861 began was Brevet Major General David E. Twiggs, a distinguished but superannuated Georgian. Twiggs had entered the army at the beginning of the War of 1812 and his commendable service brought him a brigadier general's star during the Mexican War. In 1861, however, Twiggs was seventy years old and long past his prime.

Twiggs did not resign his commission when Georgia seceded. Instead he retained command of the largest United States Army force and then surrendered it without resistance or protest to the revolutionary Texans. Although the senior United States officer to cast his lot with the Confederacy, Twiggs did not accept a regular commission, probably because of age. He subsequently served as major general in the Provisional Army until his infirmaties forced his retirement in early 1862.

The unexpected surrender of the Department of Texas by General Twiggs on February 16 provided the new Confederate War Department an unexcelled opportunity to obtain a ready made regular army. The Confederates believed that a fair portion of the United States Army could be induced to go into Confederate service. There were at that time in Texas the better part of four regular regiments, the largest body of organized troops in the entire South. These forces consisted of the 2d United States Cavalry, the 1st, 3d, and 8th United States Infantry, and several batteries of the 1st and 2d United States Artillery.

Beginning in March, these widely scattered units slowly abandoned the various posts in Texas and marched to Indianola on the Gulf of Mexico, where they were to embark for the North. The companies, which came from as far as Fort Bliss near El Paso, left behind a trail of stragglers and deserters. Earl Van Dorn had been a major in the 2d United States Cavalry stationed in Texas. The dashing little Mississippian had resigned when his state seceded and had been commissioned colonel of infantry in the Confederate regular army. On March 16, 1861, he sailed from New Orleans to Galveston and quickly proceeded down the coast to Indianola. There he met Edmund Kirby Smith and Thornton Washington who told him that many of the United States regulars gathered at Green Lake near Indianola sympathized with the South, but had not decided if they would desert to the new army.[1] Van Dorn's efforts to win these men over met with little success and they preferred to remain in Federal service. Van Dorn took the opportunity to request the Montgomery authorities to appoint Kirby Smith the lieutenant colonel of his regiment.

The Federal companies which reached Indianola by the beginning of April were safely embarked and sailed for New York or the posts in Florida still held by the Union. Van Dorn was ordered to give up his recruiting efforts and to take command of the defenses of New Orleans. But on April 12, conditions changed. Until that date the Confederate authorities hoped that secession could take place peacefully. With the firing on Fort Sumter they were confronted by a state of war. The attack on Fort Sumter changed Van Dorn's destination to Montgomery before he reached New Orleans. In the Confederate capital he received orders from General Samuel Cooper directing him to proceed immediately to Texas and to capture all the United States troops still within the state. He was at the same time given authority to enlist as many men as he could in the Confederate army.[2]

---

[1] Kirby Smith had also been a major in the 2d United States Cavalry and became lieutenant colonel of cavalry in the Confederate regular army. Washington was a first lieutenant in the 1st United States Infantry and was commissioned a captain, Adjutant General Department, in the Confederate regular army.

[2] OR, Series I, Vol. I, pp. 614-615, 623. Although Van Dorn had originally been commissioned colonel of the 2d Infantry Regiment, he was transferred to the 1st Cavalry Regiment by Special Order No. 30, A&IGO, April 20, 1861. Robert G. Hartje, Van Dorn: The Life and Times of a Confederate General (Nashville: Vanderbilt University Press, 1967), pp. 79-81; Warner, Generals in Gray, pp. 314-315.

Van Dorn moved quickly. He departed New Orleans on April 14 and swiftly captured the Federal transports off Indianola on April 17. On April 23, Van Dorn captured all the Federal troops around Indianola and on the same day the United States officers at San Antonio were seized as prisoners of war and a company of the 8th United States Infantry near the city fell into Confederate hands. This final blow completed the demoralization of the Federal units. Confederate recruiting officers, many of them recently members of these same units, made the rounds of the prisoners at Indianola. The United States officers attempted to persuade their men to remain loyal, which brought forth an order that no officer would be allowed to visit the enlisted men unless accompanied by a Confederate officer. The local newspapers were filled with arguments to show that the regulars were absolved from their allegiance because the Union was dissolved.[3]

It has always been maintained that despite the fact that a large percentage of the regular army officers joined the Confederacy, the enlisted men almost all remained loyal. This is not true in the case of the troops in Texas. In the period from February to April 1861, a total of 319 men deserted from the 1st and 3d Infantry, 2d Cavalry, and 1st and 2d Artillery in Texas. This compares with a total of only 43 for the month of January, before Texas seceded. Apparently most of these men ended up in the Confederate army. The above figures do not include the 8th United States Infantry or desertions from the organizations that were held as prisoners in Texas during May and June. It may be assumed that the total number of men who went over to the Confederates was approximately 400.[4]

Van Dorn immediately set about to implement the act passed by the Confederate Congress on March 6 by using the former United States soldiers as the nucleus for the Confederate regular army. On June 3, Van Dorn reported that he had mustered in a company of light artillery composed of old soldiers. This was Captain William Edgar's Texas Light Artillery Battery and was placed under command of Colonel Ben McCulloch to protect the northern frontier of Texas along the Red River. Van Dorn had also mustered in a company of foot artillery composed of old soldiers and ordered to Fort Bliss with instructions to throw up a field work and to defend it with

---

[3] Capt. H. M. Lazelle to Brig. Gen. L. Thomas, Jan. 4, 1862, enclosing Special Order No. 25, Headquarters, Troops in Texas, June 8, 1861, *OR,* Series II, Vol. 1, pp. 68-69. Benson J. Lossing, *Pictorial History of the Civil War* (Philadelphia: David McKay, 1866), Vol. 1, pp. 271-272. Lossing says, "They were too patriotic to be seduced, or even to listen patiently to his [Van Dorn's] wicked overtures." Hartje, *Van Dorn,* pp. 81-87.

[4] There were 2,079 enlisted men reported present for duty in the Department of Texas in January 1861, so that approximately 19.23% deserted following the secession of Texas. Returns of the Department of Texas, Office of the Adjutant General, RG 94, NA. Figures for the 8th Infantry are not included because of the poor condition of the original returns and muster rolls. Bvt. Maj. Gen. Emory Upton, *Military Policy of the United States,* p. 239, has the amazing statement that only twenty-six enlisted men were known to have joined the rebellion. No source is given for this number. It is unfortunate that this figure is repeated even recently in Coffman, *The Old Army,* p. 205, and E. B. Long, *The Civil War Day by Day* (Garden City: Doubleday & Co., Inc., 1971), p. 709.

the six pieces of artillery there. This unit was probably Captain Trevanion T. Teel's Light Battery B, 1st Texas Artillery Regiment. Why both these units formed from former United States soldiers were Texas organizations rather than part of the Confederate regular army is uncertain. Teel's Battery subsequently took part in Sibley's New Mexico campaign.[5]

In addition to these two Texas organizations, two regular army units were formed from the deserters in Texas: Haskell's detachment of recruits for a regular infantry regiment, and a company for the cavalry regiment. The Confederate regular cavalry was supposed to consist of two regiments, each having a colonel, a lieutenant colonel, a major, and ten companies. The companies consisted of a captain, a first lieutenant, two

**EARL VAN DORN
MAJOR GENERAL, C.S.A.**
*Wood Engraving from Frank Leslie's
Illustrated Magazine, June 6, 1863.
Courtesy of the Museum of the Confederacy*

second lieutenants, four sergeants, four corporals, one farrier, one blacksmith, two musicians, and sixty privates. Each cavalry regiment was to have an adjutant selected from one of the lieutenants, a sergeant major selected from the enlisted men, and a quartermaster sergeant who was added on May 16, 1861.[6]

The cavalry company was placed under the command of 1st Lieutenant Edward Ingraham, a former officer of the 1st United States Cavalry and one of the most active Confederate recruiters at Indianola. Ingraham had been born in Pennsylvania, but had received a direct commission in the 1st United States Cavalry from Mississippi in 1856. He received his appointment in the Confederate service from South Carolina.

Van Dorn was able to report the formation of the cavalry company as early as April 27, but it was not until May 1 that Ingraham was officially placed in command and 2d Lieutenant John Bradley, Confederate States In-

---

[5] *OR,* Series I, Vol. I, p. 573. Martin Hardwick Hall, *Sibley's New Mexico Campaign* (Austin: University of Texas Press, 1960), pp. 321-322.

[6] *Statutes,* Chapter XXIV, Sections 7 and 8, and Chapter XX, Section 6.

fantry, assigned to temporary duty with the company. The new unit was designated Company A, Confederate States Cavalry, and ordered to San Antonio. This was to be the first company of the 1st Confederate Cavalry. Van Dorn was colonel of the regiment with Kirby Smith as lieutenant colonel and Richard H. Anderson as major. The captains included Nathan G. Evans, J. E. B. Stuart, John Pegram, and John B. Hood.[7]

The company had been organized on the promise to the men that the Confederate government would meet the back pay and allowances which they had forfeited by deserting from the United States service, and that the term of enlistment would be for the unexpired portion of their last United States enlistment. Cooper admitted to Van Dorn that he could not positively say the Confederate government would live up to this agreement, but he thought President Davis was in favor of it and Van Dorn should do his best to get accurate copies of the men's United States Army records.[8]

The demoralization resulting from the surrender presented the Confederate company officers with disciplinary problems. On May 8, Private Thomas Fitzgerald, late of the 3d United States Infantry, became staggering drunk in the company quarters at San Antonio and attempted to shoot Corporal John Ramsey, late of the 1st United States Infantry. Fitzgerald received thirty days hard labor for his trouble. Interestingly, both remained with Company A until the Nashville campaign in late 1864.[9]

On June 8, the company was ordered to take all the Federal prisoners in San Antonio and establish a camp for them on the Salado River which flowed southward just east of the town. The Federal officers were relieved from all further control over their men. This was another obvious attempt by Van Dorn to induce the men to desert and join the Confederate ranks.

The first company muster roll, prepared on June 30 at Camp Van Dorn, as the new post was called, showed that the company was almost up to authorized strength. There were on the roll one of the three officers, all four sergeants, four corporals, and two buglers, and fifty-five of the sixty-two privates authorized by the Act of March 6. Three privates had already deserted. A few of the men were Texans who had signed up for the Confederate regular army tour of either three or five years, but the great majority of the men were former United States regulars.

---

[7] Van Dorn to Cooper, April 27, 1861, Register of Letters Received, A&IGO, Chap. I, Vol. 45, p. 241; Special Order No. 2, Headquarters, Troops in Texas, May 1, 1861; RG 109, NA. The designation of the company became Company A, 1st Confederate Cavalry, when the second regiment was authorized on May 16, 1861.

[8] Cooper to Van Dorn, May 24, 1861, Letters Received, Department of Texas, RG 109, NA.

[9] General Order No. 7, Headquarters, Troops in Texas, May 22, 1861, RG 109, NA.

The United States Army safely out of the way, the immediate problem facing Van Dorn was growing Indian unrest. With the abandonment of the frontier posts by the United States Army, the Indians were again attacking the scattered settlements and ranches. On July 21, Ingraham, with four non-commissioned officers and twenty-five privates, was ordered to the ranch of Marcellus French on the Atascosa River south of San Antonio where recent Indian depredations had been committed. If he discovered that the Indians had been more recently on the Medina, closer to town, he was to exercise discretion in first pursuing them, but in any case was to "chastise" them. Richardson's company of the 2d Texas Mounted Rifles, stationed to the west of Fort Inge, was to cooperate in this movement.[10] The result of this expedition is not recorded, but it is typical of service performed by Company A during this period.

On August 17, Company A was ordered to escort the prisoners of war from Camp Van Dorn to Camp Verde, some sixty miles northwest of San Antonio, and turn them over to the officer commanding the post. Camp Verde, established in 1856, is mainly famous for its part in the camel experiment of the pre-war army and these unpopular animals were still there when the prisoners arrived. Lieutenant Bradley then was to return to San Antonio and take charge of the eight piece howitzer battery and then report to Brigadier General H. H. Sibley for duty. The last part of the order apparently was revoked and the company missed being part of Sibley's command bound for New Mexico.[11] The company broke camp and moved to its old barracks in San Antonio on September 1. That afternoon for the last time in Texas they were paraded and inspected by Van Dorn on the square adjoining the Alamo.[12]

At the beginning of the Civil War there were three distinct military installations in San Antonio. The historic Alamo was used only as a quartermaster depot. On the west side of town San Antonio Arsenal had recently been established. The garrison of the post was quartered in San Antonio Barracks, located on the Military Plaza. San Antonio Barracks which had been garrisoned up to that time by 1st Lieutenant Alexander M. Haskell's detachment of regular infantry. This unit had not been a success and the hoped for infantry regiment never materialized. Haskell had been a lieutenant in Company K, 1st United States Infantry, before his resignation. It may be assumed that it was mainly due to him and to Sergeant William Barrett, now

---

[10] Special Order No. 43, Department of Texas, July 21, 1861, RG 109, NA. Stephen B. Oates, *Confederate Cavalry West of the River* (Austin: University of Texas Press, 1961), p. 8.

[11] Special Order No. 57, Department of Texas, August 17, 1861, RG 109, NA. Hall, *Sibley's New Mexico Campaign*, pp. 32-34. Herbert M. Hart, *Old Forts of the Southwest* (New York: Bonanza Books, 1964), pp. 52-53.

[12] Special Order No. 69, Department of Texas, August 30, 1861, RG 109, NA.

of Company A, that twenty-four enlisted men of that company had been induced to join the Confederates. But besides commanding the detachment, Haskell had also been acting as post commander, quartermaster, commissary, and any other staff officer needed. The detachment consisted of only thirteen men and it was decided to break it up and let Haskell spend full time on his staff duties. Haskell served later as major of the 6th Texas Infantry and then became assistant adjutant general on the staffs of Van Dorn, Breckinridge, Beauregard, and Withers. Two of the enlisted men were court-martialed and deserted. Two were transferred to Capt. William Edgar's Texas Light Artillery Battery which was composed almost exclusively of old United States regulars. The sergeant was discharged at the end of his old enlistment and the remaining five men were attached to Company A. This temporary attachment proved even more permanent than that of Lieutenant Bradley.

Van Dorn, by now a brigadier general in the Provisional Army, was relieved from command of the Department of Texas early in September and ordered to duty with the army in Virginia. He was temporarily succeeded by Colonel Henry McCulloch, 1st Texas Mounted Rifles. McCulloch, the older brother of Ben McCulloch, served most of the war in Texas.[13]

On September 9, Company A received orders to march to Fort Inge to relieve Richardson's Texans as garrison of the post. The company left San Antonio on September 13, completing the ninety mile march to Fort Inge on September 17.[14] Ingraham had spent too much time in remote frontier posts in the Old Army to want to sit out the war in a backwater like Fort Inge. He submitted his resignation as company commander on August 29, and left to join Van Dorn in Virginia. Command of the company reverted to Bradley, who found himself the only officer within ninety miles of Fort Inge.

Fort Inge, established in 1849, was located on the left bank of the Leona River near the present town of Uvalde. The post had been of considerable importance because of its location on the great inland commercial route at the point where the lower El Paso — San Antonio road branched off the Eagle Pass. It had been abandoned by the Federals on March 19 and promptly occupied by Texas troops. The post consisted of a dozen buildings of various sizes scattered about the border of a parade ground which was pleasantly shaded by hackberries and elms.[15]

The first month at Fort Inge was uneventful. During the second week

---

[13] Warner, *Generals in Gray*, p. 201.

[14] Post Return, Ft. Inge, Texas, September 1861, RG 109, NA.

[15] Robert W. Frazer, *Forts of the West* (Norman: University of Oklahoma Press, 1965), p. 152; Hart, *Old Forts of the Southwest*, pp. 47-48.

of October, however, a raid by hostile Indians caused Bradley to send out a scouting party. Being the only officer present, Bradley was forced to remain at the post, but on the evening of October 11, Sergeant William Barrett with two noncommissioned officers and fifteen privates left the fort, taking four days' rations: They soon discovered that the hostiles were headed westward for the Neuces River. Barrett immediately gave chase, camping that night on the Rio Frio.

Early the next morning they struck the trail of the Indians between the Rio Frio and Leona and continued to follow it until dark. The pursuit continued on October 13, the trail now heading for Fort Yulee. That night two mules and two ponies with arrows sticking out of them staggered into camp and died. On Monday, October 14, the pursuit resumed, but the trail was lost after about half a mile. After some back tracking, Barrett discovered that the Indians were retracing their steps toward the Rio Grande.

The trail crossed back and forth across Barosito Creek as the troops pressed on in a steady rain. Many of the crossings were boggy, causing the horses to become stuck and the ammunition wet. Much time was wasted in pulling the animals free with lariats. About sunset the detachment arrived at a small clearing and Corporal Kasimir Kraus and Privates William Gibbons and Peter Gernhardt dismounted. Suddenly the surrounding scrub was alive with Lipan Indians. The troopers had blundered into the Indian camp.

The men immediately unslung their carbines and tried to put up a fight, but not one in half a dozen would fire despite the use of four or five caps. The drenching suffered during the day had made the guns and ammunition completely unfit for action. The troopers resorted to their sabres, one of the few times in the American Indian wars this weapon saw service, and the three dismounted men engaged in hand to hand battle with the hostiles, killing several. The fight lasted for about half an hour. The three dismounted men were dead, Private George Smith and four of the horses had been wounded and more Indians were arriving every minute. Barrett wisely decided to call a retreat. In the desperate encounter his men had killed about ten Indians and wounded several more.[16]

On Tuesday morning the battered detachment headed back to the fort, arriving on the evening of October 16. Bradley reported bitterly that being the only commissioned officer at the post, he was unable to lead a fresh expedition to recover the bodies of the dead troopers and properly chastise the

---

[16] Report of Barrett to Bradley, October 16, 1861, *OR*, Series I, Vol. IV, pp. 33-34. The troops might have been somewhat surprised by D. Alexander Brown's statement in *The Galvanized Yankees* (Urbana: University of Illinois Press, 1963), p. 211, that since the Confederacy never engaged in war with Indian tribes, its government could not offer prisoners of war their freedom in exchange for frontier service.

Indians. McCulloch relented and assigned 2d Lieutenant James P. Baltzell, Confederate States Infantry, to temporary duty with the company. Baltzell, a Texan and an 1860 graduate of Virginia Military Institute, had already served a couple of short details with Company A and was now to be "temporarily" attached to it for over a year.

There was no further major trouble with the Indians, but Bradley was again faced with the problem of maintaining discipline. On November 13, he tossed Privates John Meara, Brinton Miles, Thomas McCarthy, Martin Monahan, and George Wright into the guard house and forwarded court-martial charges to department headquarters in Galveston. Bradley's request for a court-martial was turned down on the grounds that it would be injurious to the interests of the service to convene a court-martial at so remote a place as Fort Inge. It was suggested that he convene a garrison court-martial. Since Bradley and Baltzell were the only officers at the post this was not legally possible. On December 13, Bradley requested that the charges be withdrawn since the men had already spent a month in the guard house and there was no likelihood of a court-martial being organized in the near future.[17]

Near the end of December, Bradley received orders from McCulloch, now commanding the Western District of the Department of Texas, relieving the company from duty at Fort Inge and sending it back to San Antonio. A lack of transportation delayed the move until the first week of January 1862, but then the company marched to San Antonio and again occupied its old quarters at San Antonio Barracks.

While Company A had been isolated at its small outpost on the frontier, the war in the East had been getting into full swing. Van Dorn, now a major general, had been ordered from Virginia to join Major General Sterling Price in Missouri. On January 15, 1862, probably on his suggestion, the War Department ordered Ingraham to return to Texas, take command of Company A, and bring it to Van Dorn in Arkansas.

The following day Ingraham wrote to General Cooper regarding an unsettled obligation to the company:

> ...Company A, C.S. Cavalry, which I enlisted and organized, has not to my knowledge been paid its back pay which was promised them by me under verbal authority from Maj. Gen. Earl Van Dorn. They were promised all the back pay due them by the U.S. government and the extra pay for re-enlistment in that service — their whole contract with that government in fact being transferred to the Confederate States. Being

---

[17] Bradley to Capt. D. C. Stith, November 22, 1861; Maj. Samuel Boyer Davis to Bradley, December 9 and 12, 1861, Letters Sent, Department of Texas, Chap. II, Vol. 135, pp. 29, 42; Bradley to Davis, December 13, 1861, Letters Received, Department of Texas; RG 109, NA.

under orders to join my company, I would like this matter settled and an order given for the payment of these men previous to their being moved to Missouri.

Secretary of War Judah P. Benjamin was of the opinion that he had no power to make any such payments, but if a complete statement of what was due to the men could be furnished, he would ask Congress for permission to pay what had been promised. Apparently the men never did get the money due to them.[18]

Ingraham reached San Antonio from Richmond on February 24 and succeeded Bradley in command of the company. The company had moved from San Antonio Barracks to a camp six miles out of town on the Salado River. Ingraham found the company in good shape and well armed with Sharps carbines and sabres. The one thing that worried him was their uniforms. These were in good condition, but unfortunately were blue and he was afraid the men would be mistaken for Yankees the first time they went into battle.[19]

By the time the company finally started east, the situation had changed dramatically for the worse. Van Dorn's dream of reconquering Missouri had ended in bloody defeat at Pea Ridge in northern Arkansas and the battered Confederate army was now stretched along the Arkansas and White Rivers in an attempt to cover Little Rock and the approaches to Memphis. But if the situation west of the Mississsippi was bad, that east of the river was rapidly turning into disaster. Grant had opened the route of invasion along the Tennessee and Cumberland Rivers with the conquest of Forts Henry and Donelson, Nashville had fallen, and the main Confederate army had suffered a bloody repulse at Shiloh. General Beauregard had fallen back to Corinth in northern Mississippi and now sent frantic appeals for reinforcements.

Troops from Texas for Van Dorn's now vanished invasion of Missouri began arriving in Arkansas during the first part of April. Company A was camped on April 13 seven miles from Lewisburg on the Arkansas River northwest of Little Rock.[20] But orders had come from Van Dorn to move his entire army east of the Mississippi by way of Memphis to join Beauregard, leaving behind only a small covering force in Arkansas. On April 15, In-

---

[18] Special Order No. 15, A&IGO, January 15, 1862; Igraham to Cooper, January 16, 1862, Letters Received, A&IGO; RG 109, NA.

[19] Muster Roll, Company A, 1st Confederate Regular Cavalry, February 28, 1862, RG 109, NA.

[20] This information is found, interestingly enough, on a property voucher for a dead mule. *CMSR*, 2d Lt. James P. Baltzell, Staff File, RG 109, NA.

graham received orders to immediately proceed with Company A to Memphis and report to Van Dorn for duty.[21]

On April 25, Van Dorn promoted Ingraham to major in the Provisional Army. Although this was a staff appointment, Ingraham immediately was assigned to duty commanding a temporary cavalry battalion consisting of Company A, Captain Thomas Reve's Company of Scouts, and another separate company. This battalion served directly under Van Dorn, and Bradley once more assumed command of Company A.[22]

Van Dorn's army was not to remain in Memphis long. By May 4 he had completed the movement to Corinth and had joined Beauregard. The Union pressure already was building up and the siege lines drawing closer to the city. On May 9, Van Dorn led a counterattack against a portion of the Union line east of the city at Farmington commanded by Major General John Pope. After skirmishing all day, the Federals withdrew from the village. A cotton gin and a bridge were burned and then the Confederates also withdrew. Losses in Van Dorn's command had been light, only nine men being killed, but Company A suffered its first loss of the war. Major Edward Ingraham fell mortally wounded at Farmington while carrying despatches for Van Dorn and died the next day, deeply mourned by his general.[23]

After the evacuation of Corinth on May 30, Company A was permanently assigned as escort for Van Dorn and fell back with his army to Priceville, near Tupelo, and finally to Vicksburg, when he was assigned to command the Department of Southern Mississippi and East Louisiana on June 20, 1862. The company was now down to an aggregate strength of fifty-eight officers and men.[24] During the summer, Company A was in Vicksburg while the garrison of that city under Van Dorn's leadership repulsed the first Union effort to cut the Confederacy in two. Another fragment of the regular army was at Vicksburg at the same time. Company I, 1st Louisiana Heavy Artillery, had originally been formed as Company E, Infantry School of Practice, at Baton Rouge in 1861. Following the evacuation of New Orleans, this unit had been transferred to Vicksburg.

In September, Lieutenant Baltzell was relieved from duty with the company. Baltzell eventually became a captain in the Provisional Army, serving

---

[21] Special Order No. 52, Trans-Mississippi District, Department No. 2, April 15, 1862, *OR,* Series I, Vol. XIII, p. 818. Hartje, *Van Dorn,* p. 166; Oates, *Confederate Cavalry West of the River,* pp. 34, 36-37.

[22] Special Order No. 65, Army of the West, April 25, 1862, and Return, Army of the West, May 4, 1862, RG 109, NA.

[23] *OR,* Series I, Vol. X, Part 1, p. 808. Hartje, *Van Dorn,* pp. 177-179.

[24] Return, District of Mississippi, July 1862, *OR,* Series I, Vol. XVII, Part 2, p. 661, and Muster Rolls, Company A, 1st Confederate Regular Cavalry, July 1, 1862, and August 31, 1862, RG 109, NA.

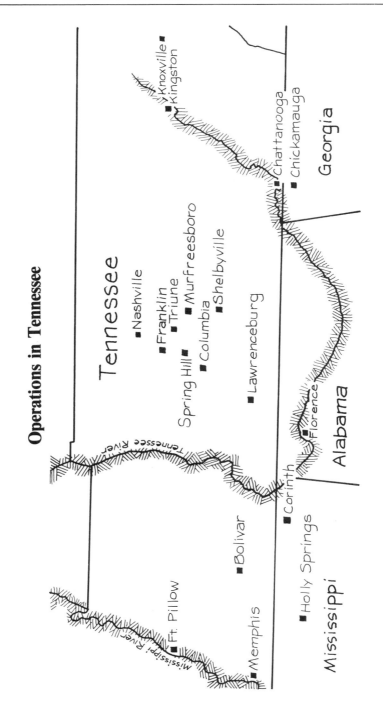

Operations in Tennessee

mainly on provost marshal duty, and was paroled with the Army of Tennessee at the end of the war. Before the end of the year two enlisted men assigned to the 1st Louisiana Heavy Artillery who had originally enlisted in the Infantry School of Practice and had survived the debacle of the fall of New Orleans were transferred to Company A.[25] Bradley was also promoted to captain in the Provisional Army in recognition of his long command of the company.

In the fall of 1862, Van Dorn and Price combined their commands to threaten the growing Union forces in West Tennessee. Accompanied by Company A, Van Dorn's army launched a disastrous attack on Corinth on October 3 and 4. Following his defeat, Van Dorn withdrew through Oxford and Coffeeville to Abbeville, skirmishing with the enemy cavalry. Only prompt action by Company A saved Van Dorn and his staff from being captured at Water Valley on December 4 when they were surrounded by the enemy in a small hotel in the town.[26] The retreat finally ended at Grenada on December 6.

As a result of the defeat at Corinth, Van Dorn was relieved of command of the district. In early December he was ordered to form a cavalry expedition to disrupt Grant's preparations to attack Vicksburg from the interior of the state. On December 16, Company A began the great cavalry raid with the rest of Van Dorn's force. The raiders surprised and captured Holly Springs on December 20, destroying a huge Union supply base. Then they swept up the Mobile and Ohio Railroad. In a sharp action at Davis's Mills, the Confederates were repulsed from the bridge over the Wolf River, Company A losing one private wounded and captured. After another skirmish at Middleburg, Tennessee, the raiders circled Bolivar and returned to their base at Grenada on December 28. Two enlisted men of Company A apparently deserted during the action at Middleburg.[27]

On January 13, 1863, Van Dorn took command of the cavalry of the Department of Mississippi and East Louisiana. Company A from this time until the end of war participated in the major cavalry campaigns of the West. General Joseph E. Johnston ordered the concentration of most of the cavalry in the West to operate with General Braxton Bragg's army in Middle Tennessee. Van Dorn's cavalry corps began a cold and miserable march from Tupelo by way of Florence, Alabama, and joined the Army of Tennessee at

---

[25] Richard P. Weinert, "The Confederate Regulars in Louisiana," *Louisiana Studies*, Vol. VI, No. 1 (Spring 1967), pp. 53-71. Special Orders No. 69 and 70, Army of the District of Mississippi, RG 109, NA.

[26] Hartje, *Van Dorn*, p. 253.

[27] Muster Roll, Company A, 1st Confederate Regular Cavalry, November 30, 1861, to December 31, 1862, RG 109, NA. Hartje, *Van Dorn*, pp. 257-267.

Columbia, Tennessee, on February 20. Making his headquarters at Spring Hill, southwest of Franklin, Van Dorn assumed command of the combined cavalry force and screened the left wing of the Confederate army. From late February to early May there were many clashes in the area, the most significant being the battles at Thompson's Station on March 5 and Franklin on April 10.

Van Dorn during his life was a controversial figure and he remains so today. A brilliant cavalry officer, he was a disappointment in command of large combined forces. Weaknesses of his personal character, however, have done the most damage to his reputation. Apparently at Spring Hill he became involved in an affair with the wife of Dr. George B. Peters. Although the exact circumstances are still shrouded in mystery, there is no

**FRANK C. ARMSTRONG
BRIGADIER GENERAL, C.S.A.**
*Courtesy of Eleanor S. Brockenbrough
Library, The Museum of the Confederacy
Richmond, Virginia*

doubt that on the morning of May 7, Peters entered Van Dorn's office and assassinated the general. It appears that pursuit of the murderer may have been delayed because of the absence of Company A from headquarters that morning. The company performed its last service for its colonel by escorting his body to Columbia the following day.[28]

On May 18, Company A was assigned as the personal escort of Brigadier General Frank C. Armstrong. The following record of events from the muster roll of Company A illustrates the service of the Company during this period:

> May 8, Company A escorted remains of Gen. Van Dorn to Columbia; May 9, returned to Springfield [Spring Hill]. May 18, attached to Gen. Armstrong's Brigade as Escort to the General. May 29, left Springfield. May 30, marched 48 miles; May 31, marched 22 miles. June 1, marched 22 miles, camped near Lawrenceburg. June 2, marched 20 miles, camped near Mount Pleasant. June 3, marched 12 miles, camped near Columbia. June 4, marched 11 miles, camped near Springfield. June 5, marched 12 miles, fight near Franklin. June 6, marched 18 miles, camped near Springfield. June 7, left camp 8 o'clock P.M., marched 8 miles, June

---

[28] *Ibid.*, p. 316.

8, left camp 4 o'clock A.M., skirmish at Truin[e] 3 P.M. June 11, skirmish at Triaon [sic]. June 12, arrived at Springfield 10 P.M., heavy weather. June 13, camped near Springfield. June 25, left Springfield. June 26, camped near Unionville. June 27, skirmish at Shelbyville. June 28, camped near Tullahoma. June 29, camped near Dehar Station. June 30, camped Arazona, (East Tennessee).[29]

Following the death of Van Dorn, Brigadier General Nathan Bedford Forrest was sent to Spring Hill to take over command of the cavalry of the Army of Tennessee. Forrest assigned Company A as escort to Armstrong. Armstrong, who had been directly commissioned in the 2d United States Dragoons, commanded a Union cavalry company at First Manassas. He resigned in August 1861 and was appointed a second lieutenant in the 1st Confederate Regular Cavalry even though he had been a captain in the United States Army, probably because all of the higher vacancies had been filled. Armstrong was one of the best young cavalry leaders and quickly rose of the rank of brigadier general and in 1863 commanded one of Forrest's brigades.[30]

**NATHAN BEDFORD FORREST
LIEUTENANT GENERAL, C.S.A.**
*Museum of the Confederacy,
Courtesy of The Library of Congress*

Perhaps the hardest battle of the war for Company A was the little known engagement near Franklin on June 4, 1863, mentioned in the record of events above erroneously as occurring on June 5. At 3 p.m. on the afternoon of June 4 the First Brigade, First Cavalry Division, of the Army of the Cumberland made contact with pickets' of Armstrong's Brigade about a mile and half east of Franklin, near the Murphreesborough Road. Armstrong attacked the flank of the 2d Michigan Cavalry and in turn was charged by the 6th Kentucky Cavalry (Union). His troops fell back across the Harpeth River and then crossed the Lewisburg Pike. The 2d Michigan Cavalry then dismounted and deployed as skirmishers along the center of the line with the

---

[29] Muster Roll, Company A, 1st Confederate Regular Cavalry, dated June 30, 1863, RG 109, NA. The roll shows one officer and forty-six enlisted men.

[30] Robert S. Henry, *"First With the Most"* Forrest (Indianapolis and New York: Bobbs-Merrill Co., 1944), p. 161. Warner, *Generals in Gray*, pp. 12-13, and Regular Army Register, Chap. I, Vol. 88, p. 60, RG 109, NA.

4th Kentucky Cavalry (Union) to its left and the 9th Pennsylvania Cavalry covering the flanks.

Finally the 4th Kentucky charged while the 2d Michigan attacked the center of Armstrong's line. Armstrong fell back, but the Union troops managed to turn his left flank, forcing a hasty retreat. By this time it was completely dark and, in the confusion, the Confederates disengaged and made good their withdrawal. In the fierce hand to hand fighting, the flag and four troopers of Company A were captured. Armstrong and seventeen men of Company A were briefly in the hands of the enemy, but all but the four enlisted men managed to escape in the dark.[31]

On June 14, one of the troopers of Company A became involved in a strange affair. A dispute between Forrest and Lieutenant A. Willis Gould resulted in the lieutenant attacking the general. Forrest stabbed Gould, who fled the room. The lieutenant took refuge in another building and two doctors were examining Gould's wound when Forrest stormed in the front door. Gould ran out into an alley behind the building and started to run. Forrest, in hot pursuit, fired at him and missed, the ball ricocheting and striking one of the troopers of Company A, mentioned only as "a Dutchman of Armstrong's escort," in the fleshy part of the leg. The lieutenant soon died of his original wound. Unfortunately, it is impossible to identify the name of the soldier of Company A.[32]

During the remainder of the summer, Company A, with the remainder of Forrest's cavalry, screened the front of the Army of Tennessee in Middle Tennessee. With the withdrawal of the army to Chattanooga, Forrest's troops were stationed along the Tennessee River to cover General Bragg's right flank. Following the retreat from Chattanooga, Forrest's cavalry actively and effectively scouted the Union advance into Georgia. From the area of Ringgold, Georgia, Armstrong's Brigade on September 18 was ordered to cover the front of Polk's Corps during the operations that led to the Battle of Chickamauga on September 19 and 20. For most of those two days, Forrest's troops fought dismounted in attacks against the northern part of the Federal line. The charges made by Armstrong's men were praised by Forrest as "creditable to the best drilled infantry." On September 21, following the fleeing enemy, Forrest was riding with Armstrong. Spying some Federal cavalry, Forrest immediately gave chase as the enemy fired a volley and hastily retreated. By the time Forrest called a halt to the pursuit, the men of Company A were sitting their horses on top of Missionary Ridge looking down on Chattanooga.[33]

---

[31] *OR*, Series I, Vol. XXIII, Part 1, pp. 359-362. Eric William Sheppard, *Beford Forrest: The Confederacy's Greatest Cavalryman* (London: H.F. & G. Witherby, 1930), p. 121.

[32] Henry, *Forrest*, pp. 161-163.

[33] *OR*, Series I, Vol. XXX, Part 1, p. 525 and Part 4, pp. 65, 663. Henry, *Forrest*, p. 191.

Following Chickamauga, the cavalry of the Army of Tennessee was reorganized and on September 24 Armstrong's Brigade was ordered to report to the command of Major General Joseph Wheeler. Two days later Armstrong reported to Wheeler from near Charleston, Tennessee, that his command was unable to start on an expedition across the mountains. His horses needed shoeing and his men had been without rations for thirty-six hours.[34]

On November 2, Captain Bradley requested that Company A be transferred back to Texas before the enlistments of most of the men expired on April 25, 1864. It was apparent that under the terms of the Conscript Act the men would be held in service after the expiration of their enlistments and they requested that in such case they be allowed to serve under the command of General E. Kirby Smith, who as lieutenant colonel of the 1st Confederate Regular Cavalry had succeeded to the titular head of the regiment on the death of Van Dorn. Armstrong forwarded the application with the endorsement: "Disapproved. This Co. only has about 28 men left & is now on duty at my Hd. Qrs. as couriers, etc.- Respectfully request the Co. may be left where it is." The request was not approved by General Bragg and so the company remained east of the Mississippi for the duration.[35]

Armstrong's troops were once again ready for action when Wheeler crossed the Tennessee River on November 13 and advanced on Maryville in support of Lieutenant General James Longstreet's campaign against Knoxville. There followed lively skirmishing near Maryville that day and a sharp action the following day which forced the Federals back to the Holston River. The enemy having been driven into the fortifications of Knoxville, Wheeler's troops took part in the siege until ordered on November 22 by Longstreet to attack Kingston. After a difficult march, Wheeler reached Kingston on November 24, but the garrison of the town beat off his attack. That day Wheeler was ordered to rejoin Bragg's army and Armstrong, given temporary command of a division, was left with the cavalry corps of Major General William T. Martin in support of Longstreet's command.[36]

Shifted back to Knoxville, Armstrong's troops crossed the Holston River below the city and demonstrated dismounted against the enemy's lines. On November 30, Armstrong's division was shifted toward Maynardsville and the following day attempted to push toward Clinch River, finally driving the

---

[34] *OR*, Series I, Vol. XXX, Part 2, p. 723, and Part 4, pp. 711, 719.

[35] Bradley to Cooper, November 2, 1863, from Clevelend, East Tennessee, *CMSR*, Capt. John Bradley, 1st Confederate Regular Cavalry, RG 109, NA. There is no record showing Kirby Smith being promoted to colonel in the regular army, although by the terms of the Act of March 6, 1861, he would have succeeded to the rank by seniority.

[36] *OR*, Series I, Vol. XXXI, Part 1, pp. 540-544. John P. Dyer, *From Shiloh to San Juan* (Baton Rouge: Louisiana University Press, 1961), pp. 113-114.

enemy across the river and pursuing for several miles through gorges made difficult by a frozen stream. Longstreet began his withdrawal from Knoxville on December 2. The cavalry screened his rear and flanks as he withdrew northeast on the way back to Virginia. A sharp skirmish took place near Bean's Station on December 11. On December 22, Martin's corps returned across the Holston, and Armstrong's division was concentrated at Talbot's Depot, on the road leading from Morristown to New Market. On the morning of December 24, the Federals attacked Armstrong and Colonel A.A. Russell's brigade. After spirited skirmishing, Armstrong, flanked and outnumbered, withdrew his pickets from near New Market to the east side of Mossy Creek. Fierce fighting continued in the area during the following days. On December 29, Martin engaged the enemy on both sides of the railroad from Mossy Creek to Morristown. Armstrong's division held the enemy's attention, but a flanking attack with Brigadier General John T. Morgan's force was thwarted by the withdrawal of the Federals. The Federals soon counterattacked and after a fierce fight the Confederates, running low on ammunition, were forced to withdraw.[37]

Having covered Longstreet's withdrawal from Knoxville, Martin's cavalry began to move southwest to rejoin the Army of Tennessee. On January 27, 1864, the Federals under Brigadier General Samuel Sturgis struck Martin's command inflicting a serious defeat near Fair Garden, about ten miles east of Sevierville. The following day Armstrong was able to repulse the pursuit. Armstrong then went on leave and was subsequently ordered to report to Major General Stephen D. Lee, commanding cavalry under the control of Lieutenant General Leonidas Polk. Polk, in turn, ordered him in March to report once again to Forrest, but this transfer did not take place. Apparently Company A accompanied Armstrong when he left East Tennessee, because records continue to show it as his escort until after the Nashville Campaign.[38]

Armstrong's command apparently spent April in northern Alabama chasing deserters. Captain Bradley, however, had had enough. On May 2, 1864, he requested transfer to the Trans-Mississippi Department. The War Department agreed to this with the provision that he resign his Provisional Army commission and revert to his regular army rank of second lieutenant. Bradley complied and finished the war on staff duty in Texas as a lieutenant. Command of Company A devolved upon 2d Lieutenant John Denys who had been first sergeant of the company before he was commissioned in the regular army on September 23, 1863.[39]

---

[37] *OR*, Series I, Vol. XXXI, Part 1, pp. 545-548, 630-632, 639-641.

[38] *Ibid.*, Vol. XXXII, Part 1, pp. 34, 131, 132, 134-136, 140, 143, 150; Part 2, p. 681; Part 3, pp. 588, 616, 668.

[39] Bradley to Cooper, May 2, 1864, from Tuscaloosa, Ala. Bradley submitted his resignation on August 10, 1864, from East Point, Ga. *CMSR*, Capt. John Bradley, 1st Confederate Cavalry, and Regular Army Register, Chap. I, Vol. 88, RG 109, NA.

On May 12, 1864, Armstrong's Brigade was assigned as part of General Polk's Army of the Mississippi and two days later was attached to Brigadier General William H. Jackson's cavalry division. The cavalry skirmished near Rome, Georgia, on May 15 and then was transferred to the Army of Tennessee on May 22. Armstrong's Brigade took part in the severe fighting around Atlanta, mainly being employed to screen the army to the south and southwest of the city. After the fall of Atlanta on September 1, Armstrong moved with the Army of Tennessee north of the city in an attempt to cut Sherman's line of communications. On September 26, Armstrong reported that out of one officer and forty men of Company A, thirty men were barefooted. In early October the brigade was operating around New Hope Church and then began withdrawing westward into Alabama, reaching Tuscumbia on November 4.[40]

General John B. Hood now prepared to take a desperate gamble. Sherman had started him March to the Sea, and Hood rather than attempting to oppose him, swung the Army of Tennessee west and north and advanced on Nashville. Forrest assumed command of all of the cavalry and Jacksons Division's crossed the Tennessee River at Florence on November 16 and 17. After bivouacking at Shoal Creek, Jackson's Division advanced on the morning of November 21 toward Lawrenceburg and then southeast in the direction of Pulaski. Armstrong's Brigade was in the lead and skirmished constantly with the enemy. Passing through Lawrenceburg, he then encountered Hatch's Union cavalry division and captured 100 of the enemy after a short engagement. The Confederate cavalry reached Columbia on November 24 and invested the town until relieved by infantry on November 27. The next morning, Jackson crossed the Duck River at Holland's Ford and proceeded to the vicinity of Hurt's Cross Roads on the Lewisburg Pike. On November 29, Jackson moved along the pike toward Franklin to develop the enemy. Armstrong made contact with the Federals, but was ordered not to press them until Forrest reached the flank. The Union troops fell back skirmishing to Spring Hill and Armstrong was ordered to form a line of battle. He then charged the enemy, but was repulsed. The Federals hurriedly retreated as Forrest kept up the pressure, sending Jackson toward Thompson's Station to intercept the withdrawal. At 11 p.m., Jackson reached the road at Fitzgerald, four miles from Spring Hill, and attacked the head of the retreating column. The fight lasted until near daylight and the Confederates succeeded in burning several wagons.

The next day the pursuit continued down the Franklin Pike until the enemy was driven into the defenses of the town. Jackson crossed the Harpeth

---

[40] OR, Series I, Vol. XXXVIII, Part 4, pp. 704, 710, 714, 735, 739, Part 5, pp. 879, 898; and Vol. XXXIX, Part 2, p. 514.

River and skirmished with the enemy until he withdrew back across the river in the evening to replenish ammunition. On December 1, Forrest crossed the Harpeth and struck the Federals at Owen's Cross Roads. Jackson's Division then moved down the Nashville Pike and camped that night near Brentwood. The following day the Confederate cavalry moved to within sight of Nashville with Jackson's Division covering the Nashville and Mill Creek Pike. Forrest began moving his cavalry down the railroad toward Murphreesborough. On December 5, Jackson's Division moved from La Vergne to attack a small fort on a hill west of Murphreesborough. The fort with eighty men and two pieces of artillery was captured and the enemy driven into the main defenses of the town.

On December 7, Union infantry advanced to relieve Murphreesborough. The Confederate infantry supporting Forrest panicked, and it took a charge by Armstrong's and Ross' brigades to halt the advance. The Federals then withdrew into Murphreesborough and things quieted down. Jackson captured and burned a train on December 16 south of the town, capturing 200 men of the 61st Illinois Infantry.

Forrest's entire command moved to Wilkinson's Cross Roads upon learning on December 16 of the crushing defeat of the Army of Tennessee at Nashville. The cavalry reached Columbia on December 18, two days later, Major General Edward C. Walthall's infantry division joined Armstrong's Brigade to act as rear guard of the retreating army. Forrest fell back across the Duck River and on December 23 halted at Lynnville to check the enemy in order to permit the escape of the wagon train and stock of the army. The following day the infantry was ordered back toward Columbia and a severe engagement ensued. Forrest then retreated two miles to Richland Creek and then advanced Armstrong's Brigade in front and Brigadier General Lawrence S. Ross' Brigade on the right flank. The Federals crossed the creek and tried to surround Forrest, but were attacked by Armstrong and Ross. Forrest then pulled back to Pulaski. On Christmas Day, Jackson covered the rear in Pulaski and burned the Richland Creek bridge after a sharp engagement. Forrest repulsed the enemy seven miles from Pulaski and camped that night at Sugar Creek. Again beating off the enemy the following day, the army finally crossed the Tennessee River at Bainbridge, Alabama, on December 27 and reached safety.[41]

The Nashville Campaign was the most disastrous of the war for Company A. On the muster roll dated October 31, 1864, there were listed one officer and forty enlisted men. Of these, one was absent without leave, eight were on detached service, and five were on extra duty. On January 1, 1865,

---

[41] *OR*, Series I, Vol. XLV, Part 1, pp. 751-759, 761-762. Henry, *Forrest*, pp. 390-416.

Corporal James Smith, commanding the remnant of the company, reported fourteen men present. Two of the men on detached service never rejoined the company, but were paroled at the end of the war. One man was captured on December 22. Lieutenant Denys deserted on December 26 and took the oath of allegiance in Nashville on January 9, 1865. Denys had enlisted at the organization of the company and by June 1861 he was first sergeant, a position he held until commissioned. He probably was an old United States regular, but any previous service has not been verified. There is no record of what happened to the remainder of the men. Armstrong's Brigade took part in much hard fighting during the period. The brigade loss is reported as 147 officers and men killed and wounded during November and December, but there is no record of the number captured or deserted.[42]

Company A reached Camargo, Mississippi, and on January 24, 1865, Forrest reorganized the cavalry and assigned Armstrong's Brigade to Brigadier General James R. Chalmer's Division. At about the same time, the remnants of Company A were consolidated with Company D, 2d Mississippi Cavalry, and served with that unit until the end of the war. Chalmer's troops, which had been shifted eastward to Priceville, Alabama, on March 22 started toward Selma with the beginning of Major General James H. Wilson's massive cavalry raid. Chalmer's advance was delayed by high water, flooded swamps, and unbridged rivers which deflected its march to the northward toward Randolph. Hearing Forrest's troops engaged with the enemy at Ebenezer Church on Six Mile Creek on March 31, part of Armstrong's Brigade came up by forced march and were put into the battle line. The Union cavalry carried the position with an overwhelming charge. Forrest then pulled back to Selma. He had only the 1,400 men of Armstrong's Brigade, Adams' militia, and fragments of Brigadier General Philip D. Roddey's and Colonel Edward Crossland's brigades to defend three and a half miles of entrenchments in front of Selma. At 5 p.m. on April 1, 9,000 Union troops smashed through the center of the Confederate line. Armstrong and Roddey, holding the flanks, were borne back by the rout and managed to cut their way out in the dark. Forrest retreated by way of Plantersville and reached Marion on April 4. He was then ordered to gather up his shattered command and went into camp at Gainesville on April 15. The war for all practical purposes was over. With the surrender of the Confederate forces commanded by Lieutenant General Richard Taylor, thirteen enlisted men — all that remained of Company A, 1st Confederate Regular Cavalry — were paroled at Columbus, Mississippi, on May 16, 1865.[43]

---

[42] Muster Rolls, Company A, 1st Confederate Regular Cavalry, dated October 31, 1861, and January 1, 1865; *CMSR*, 2d Lt. John Denys, 1st Confederate Regular Cavalry; RG 109, NA.

[43] Henry, *Forrest*, pp. 422-435. Columbus, Miss., Parole Roll No. 29, RG 109, NA.

It is impossible to tell exactly what happened to all of the eighty-six enlisted men and five officers carried at one or other time on the company muster rolls. From surviving records, it appears that one officer and four men were killed in action or died in service, although the actual number was probably higher; four men were absent as prisoners of war or had been exchanged and apparently never rejoined the company; two men were transferred; three officers and twelve men were paroled at the end of the war; and one officer and twenty-one men deserted or were last reported absent without leave. There is no final record of separation for thirty-three men, most of these disappearing about the time of the Nashville Campaign. Nine of the men paroled were former United States regulars who had served the entire war with the company. Two men had enlisted in Texas and may have also been old soldiers, but this has not been verified. The remaining trooper was a Tennessean who transferred to the company.

It had been four difficult years for Company A, beginning by fighting Indians on the frontier and ending with the final defeat of Forrest's legendary cavalry. The distance traveled by Company A during the war is remarkable. From Fort Inge, ninety miles west of San Antonio, to near Cumberland Gap, and from the area south of Atlanta to Vicksburg, Company A, 1st Confederate Regular Cavalry, maintained a commendable record of hard riding and fighting.

Chapter IV

THE LOUISIANA
REGULARS

T wo former United States military posts, a barracks and an arsenal were located at Baton Rouge. Their location on the Mississippi River, at a convenient distance from the distractions of New Orleans, made the place ideal for a general recruiting depot. Captain John C. Booth, Corps of Artillery, was assigned to command Baton Rouge Arsenal in March 1861 and also served as acting commander of Baton Rouge Barracks.

On April 5, 1861, Captain John Frazer was ordered to take command of Baton Rouge Barracks. This order was followed by two letters from General Cooper outlining Frazer's duties as superintendent of recruiting.[1] At the same time First Lieutenant Robert C. Hill was dispatched on a secret recruiting mission. Hill was to proceed to Newport, Kentucky, and St. Louis, Missouri, and attempt to induce as many old soldiers returning from the frontier as possible to join the Confederate Army.[2]

The main recruiting drive in the Mississippi Valley started, however, with the assignment on April 13 of Captain Thomas H. Taylor, Regiment of

---

[1] Special Order No. 15, A&IGO, April 5, 1861; Cooper to Frazer, April 15 and 19, 1861, Letters Sent, A&IGO, Chap. I, Vol. 35, pp. 35, 50; RG 109, NA.

[2] Cooper to Frazer, April 6, 1861; Letters Sent, A&IGO, Chap. I, Vol. 35, pp. 24-25, RG 109, NA.

Cavalry, to establish a series of recruiting rendezvous. Taylor was ordered to proceed from Montgomery to Louisville, Kentucky, by way of Memphis and Nashville. Once in Kentucky he was also to investigate the possibility of forming rendezvous at Frankfort, Lexington, Covington, and Newport.[3] Hill had established a rendezvous at Memphis and Taylor was directed to forward his recruits to Baton Rouge. On April 20, Taylor received additional help with the assignment of First Lieutenant James K. McCall to take over the station at Nashville.[4] Captain W. S. Walker and Second Lieutenant Thomas T. Grayson were ordered to Memphis to take over Hill's recruiting station.[5] Dr. John C. Nicholson of Nashville was appointed civilian recruiting agent in Middle Tennessee. The recruits were to be gathered at Nashville and forwarded to Memphis and from there to the depot at Baton Rouge Barracks.[6] Captain Frazer was still involved in various duties in New Orleans and during the first few weeks command of the recruits at Baton Rouge was exercised by Second Lieutenant Edward Powell, a former United States Army ordnance sergeant with twenty years of military experience.[7]

The recruiting station in New Orleans was commanded by First Lieutenant Charles W. Phifer, C.S. Cavalry. In an apparent attempt to try to induce more former United States regulars to desert, the steamer *Star of the West* carrying men withdrawing from Texas was detained at Fort Jackson near the mouth of the Mississippi River. Thirty-four men were left at the river forts by order of Colonel Earl Van Dorn. When they still refused First Lieutenant Edward Ingraham's enducements to enlist in the Confederate service, they were allowed to proceed to New Orleans and presumably made their way back to Union territory.[8]

On April 20, the War Department issued a requisition for $2,000 to run the depot.[9] Besides Powell, Frazer was also assigned First Lieutenant William

---

[3] Cooper to Taylor, April 13, 1861, Letters Sent, A&IGO, Chap. I, Vol. 35, p. 34. Because Kentucky at this time was officially neutral, it was necessary to carry on the recruiting in that state in secret. Lts. George B. Cosby and John B. Hood had been dispatched by the War Department on a secret mission to the Governor of Kentucky and then were to report to Taylor in Frankfort for recruiting duty. Cooper to Taylor, April 22, 1861, and Cooper to Cosby, April 23, 1861, Chap. I, Vol. 35, pp. 55, 62. Hood, however, was immediately reassigned and saw no recruiting duty. John P. Dyer, *The Gallant Hood* (Indianapolis and New York: The Bobbs-Merrill Co., Inc., 1950), pp. 48-49. Attempts at recruiting in Kentucky were soon abandoned. Cooper to 2d Lt. W. R. Bullock, May 17, 1861, and Cooper to Taylor, May 24, 1861, Chap. I, Vol. 35, pp. 122 and 141, RG 109, NA.

[4] Cooper to Frazer, April 15, 1861, and Cooper to Taylor, April 18 and 20, 1861, Letters Sent, A&IGO, Chap. I, Vol. 35, pp. 47-48, 53, RG 109, NA.

[5] Cooper to Walker, April 22, 1861, and Cooper to Taylor, April 27 and 29, 1861, Letters Sent, A&IGO, Chap. I, Vol. 35, pp. 55, 77, 79, RG 109, NA.

[6] Cooper to Nicholson, McCall, and Grayson, May 1, 1861, Letters Sent, A&IGO, Chap. I, Vol. 35, pp. 84-85. For details of the organization of the recruits at Baton Rouge, see Cooper to Frazer, April 19, 1861, Chap. I, Vol. 35, p. 50, RG 109, NA.

[7] *CMSR*, Maj. Edward Powell, Staff File; Cooper to Frazer, April 19, 1861, Letters Sent, A&IGO, Chap. I, Vol. 35, p. 50; Special Order No. 29, A&IGO, April 19, 1861; RG 109, NA.

[8] Muster Roll of Recruiting Party stationed at New Orleans, Louisiana Muster Rolls; Post Return, Forts Jackson and St. Philip, La., April 1861; RG 109, NA.

[9] Frazer to Cooper, April 17, 1861, Register of Letters Received, A&IGO, Chap. I, Vol. 45, p. 67; Cooper to Frazer, April 20, 1861, Letters Sent, A&IGO, Chap. I, Vol. 35, p. 54; RG 109, NA.

C. Porter. Porter, being senior in rank, succeeded Powell as acting commander of the depot in the absence of Frazer. On May 10, he telegraphed that he had arrested three deserters. Things apparently were not going well in Baton Rouge and on May 11 Frazer was ordered to turn over his duties in New Orleans and immediately take command in Baton Rouge.[10]

The recruits at Baton Rouge were soon numerous enough to be divided into four companies. Additional regular lieutenants were assigned to the depot to drill the men. Discipline still remained a problem, and on May 31 Frazer reported to the War Department that Private M. Kelly had been killed while resisting the corporal of the guard. Recruiting also began to drop off. Captain Taylor reported from Nashville on May 30 that recruits were unwilling to go to Baton Rouge Barracks and asked permission to establish a camp of instruction under his command. Apparently no action was taken on this request.[11]

The regular establishment was supposed to include eight infantry regiments. Each regiment of infantry was to consist of a colonel, a lieutenant colonel, a major, and ten companies. The companies were to be composed of a captain, a first lieutenant, two second lieutenants, four sergeants, four corporals, two musicians, and ninety privates.

In addition, on May 4, 1861, an act was passed authorizing a regiment of zouaves for the regular army. It was to have the same organization and in addition a sergeant major and a quartermaster sergeant, but no musicians. An additional assistant surgeon over the number authorized was included and an adjutant and quartermaster were to be selected from the lieutenants of the regiment, as in the case of the other regiments. On May 16, 1861, quartermaster sergeants were added to the line infantry regiments.

On March 20, General Cooper had written to Gaston Coppens of New Orleans accepting his battalion of zouaves for the Provisional Army. Coppens apparently went to Montgomery and discussed his battalion with President Davis and received the impression that when the act of May 4, 1861, was passed the battalion was accepted into the regular army. On May 17, Cooper ordered Brigadier General Braxton Bragg at Pensacola to muster in the battalion. Bragg was told to have the enlisted men fill out regular army enlistment papers. Something came up, of which there are no details. Four days later, Cooper wrote Bragg that the battalion would remain in service

---

[10] Special Order No. 29, A&IGO, April 19, 1862; Porter to Cooper, May 10, 11 and 12, 1861, Register of Letters Received. A&IGO, Chap. I, Vol. 45, p. 172; Cooper to Frazer, May 11, 1861, and Cooper to Porter, May 11, 1861, Letters Sent, A&IGO, Chap. I, Vol. 45, pp. 106, 108; RG 109, NA.

[11] Frazier to Cooper, May 31, 1861, and Taylor to Cooper, May 30, 1861, Register of Letters Received, Chap. I, Vol. 45, pp. 224, 70, RG 109, NA.

BATON ROUGE BARRACKS
Courtesy of Louisiana State University Libraries

ENLISTED MEN'S BARRACKS
NEW ORLEANS (JACKSON) BARRACKS
Courtesy of Louisiana Section, Louisiana State Library

for the term engaged, but no measures were to be taken to enlist the enlisted men for the regular army or organize the battalion as part of the regular force. No further discussion has been found of including the battalion in the regular army and it went on to a distinguished battle record in Virginia. None of the officers received regular commissions. The only officer appointed under the May 4, 1861, act was Camille de Polignac, who was appointed lieutenant colonel on July 6, 1861, and eventually went on to become a major general.[12]

To provide manpower for the infantry regiments, the War Department established an infantry school. Originally modeled on the United States Army system developed at the Artillery School at Fort Monroe, Virginia, in the 1820's, the Confederate Infantry School of Practice at Baton Rouge Barracks was only allowed enough time to get the men organized into companies, issue minimum equipment, and undergo the barest of training before the troops were ordered to active duty. New Orleans, the largest city and most important port in the Confederacy, in the summer of 1861, was virtually undefended. It offered a prize which the Union could not long resist.[13]

Frazer, a West Pointer and former captain in the 9th United States Infantry whose ambition was bigger than training recruits, accepted a commission as lieutenant colonel of the 8th Alabama Infantry on June 17 and left Baton Rouge. He was promoted to brigadier general in 1863, but his surrender of Cumberland Gap resulted in his appointment not being confirmed by the Senate and he spent the rest of the war as a prisoner. Frazer was succeeded by Captain Alfred Mouton. Jean Jacques Alfred Alexander Mouton was another West Pointer, but he had resigned from the army almost immediately to become an engineer in Louisiana. Despite having been out of the army for eleven years, Mouton was commissioned a captain of infantry when the Confederate regular army was formed. Mouton's connection with the Infantry School also was to be brief.

On June 19, Mouton reported that he had 417 recruits under his command. He requested additional officers and asked for instructions. Major General David Twiggs, commander of Department No. 1, was desperately searching for men for the defenses of New Orleans. Most of the troops in

---

[12] *Statutes*, Statute II, Chapters II and XX, Section 6, and Chapter XXIV, Section 3. It has been alleged that the 1st Louisiana (Coppens') Zouave Battalion was accepted into the regular army as a beginning for this regiment. Terry L. Jones, *Lee's Tigers* (Baton Rouge: Louisiana State University Press, 1987), p. 252. This is based on a letter from Maj. O. M. Watkins to Hon. John Perkins, Jr., February 25, 1865, in the Tulane University Library, which indicates that many believed during the war that the battalion had been accepted in the regular army. *OR*, Series IV, Vol. I, p. 179. All other references found to this battalion refer to it as a Louisiana unit. Regular Army Register, Vol. I, Chap. 88; Cooper to Bragg, May 17 and 21, 1861, Vol. I, Chap. 35, pp. 126, 132; RG 109, NA.

[13] For a detailed account of conditions in New Orleans and the events leading to its capture, see Charles L. Dufour, *The Night the War Was Lost* (Garden City: Doubleday & Co., Inc., 1960).

the Gulf states were tied down in the siege of Fort Pickens at Pensacola, Florida. General Cooper authorized Twiggs on June 20 to make use of the recruits at Baton Rouge.[14]

Mouton led 304 recruits to New Orleans on July 4, Powell taking command of those remaining for the time in Baton Rouge. Mouton's detachment was divided between New Orleans Barracks, three miles down the river from the city, and Fort Pike. New Orleans Barracks, established in 1834, consisted of four large permanent barracks buildings, similar to those at Baton Rouge Barracks. Fort Pike, a small brick seacoast fortification, had been constructed in the 1820's and garrisoned irregularly in the following years. Located on the west bank of Rigolets Pass twenty-five miles northeast of New Orleans, the fort guarded the eastern approach to the city. At the end of July the post returns showed Companies A, B, C, and D at New Orleans had an aggregate strength of 67, 67, 64 and 74 men respectively. The newly formed Company E at Fort Pike had an aggregate strength of 77.[15]

Mouton resigned from the regular army on July 16, becoming colonel of the 18th Louisiana Infantry and eventually a brigadier general.[16] From this date the Infantry School ceased to function as a battalion and its companies were simply designated as ''C. S. Recruits.'' Although no officer was given command of the battalion, the dominant figures apparently were Second Lieutenants J. K. Dixon and Oliver J. Semmes at New Orleans and Second Lieutenant George H. Frost at Fort Pike.[17]

Powell's detachment at Baton Rouge originally consisted of one officer and fifty-four enlisted men, but presumably since it was only to be temporarily detached from the battalion it was never given a separate company designation.[18] Included in this detachment, although also mustered separately, was the Baton Rouge hospital detail commanded by Surgeon P. M. Enders which remained at the post until the evacuation of Baton Rouge in May 1862. Powell and his detachment were ordered to join the battalion in New Orleans on September 23, leaving a sergeant and six privates behind in charge of Baton Rouge Barracks. Captain and Military Store Keeper Frederick C. Humphreys

---

[14] Mouton to Cooper, June 19, 1861, Register of Letters Received, A&IGO, Chap. I, Vol. 45, p. 285; R. H. Chilton to Twiggs, June 20, 1861, Letters Sent, A&IGO, Chap. I, Vol. 35, p. 207; Regular Army Register, Chap. I, Vol. 88; RG 109, NA. Warner, *Generals in Gray*, pp. 93, 222.

[15] Post Returns, Baton Rouge Barracks, July 1861 and July 4, 1861; New Orleans Barracks, July 1861; and Fort Pike, July 1861; RG 109, NA. *Outline Description of the Posts of the Military Division of the Missouri* (Fort Collins, Colo.: Old Army Press, 1972), pp. 211-212.

[16] Regular Army Register, Chap. I, Vol. 88, p. 127, RG 109, NA. Warner, *Generals in Gray*, pp. 222-223. The reason for his resignation from the regular army is obscure.

[17] Post Returns, New Orleans Barracks, July and August 1861; Fort Pike, July 1861. Company E was organized and so designate per Special Order No. 47, Department No. 1, July 23, 1861. RG 109, NA.

[18] Muster Roll, Powell's Detachment, Infantry School of Practice, August 31, 1861, RG 109, NA.

was ordered to Baton Rouge Arsenal on October 8 and also assumed command of Baton Rouge Barracks on October 26. Humphreys had been a Military Store Keeper in the United States Army and later served at Augusta and Columbus Arsenals in Georgia. On October 29, First Lieutenant J. H. Stith, a Provisional Army officer, received orders to assume command of Baton Rouge Barracks and the regular detachment. There was also a regular army Ordnance Detachment at Baton Rouge Arsenal commanded by Captain Booth. Booth had been a first lieutenant in the 4th United States Artillery. Commissioned a captain in the Confederate regular Corps of Artillery, he commanded Baton Rouge Arsenal until the capture of the city. Promoted to major in the Provisional Army, he next commanded Fayetteville Arsenal in North Carolina, where he died in 1862. Eleven men served at one time or another in the Baton Rouge Arsenal Ordnance Detachment. Of these, one was discharged, two were attached to the 1st Louisiana Heavy Artillery, one was attached to the Louisiana Arsenal at New Orleans, and rest disappear from the records with the fall of Baton Rouge.[19]

MAIN BUILDING, BATON ROUGE ARSENAL
Courtesy of Louisiana State University Libraries

---

[19] Edward Riley enlisted in the regular army at Memphis in May 1861 and apparently was never assigned to Baton Rouge. He appears as first sergeant of cavalry and chief clerk of the Adjutant General's Office, Polk's Corps, in November 1861. He deserted and took the oath of allegiance in Memphis in June 1864. Field Report of a Detachment of Recruits, Infantry School of Practice, September 1861; Muster Roll of Steward, Wardmaster, Cooks, and Nurses, etc., in Hospital, Baton Ruge, La., April 30, 1861; Muster Rolls, Detachment of Recruits, Army of the Confederate States, August 30, 1861, to October 31, 1861, and December 31, 1861, to May 1, 1862; filed with Louisiana Muster Rolls, RG 109, NA.

Men from the regular companies in New Orleans were detailed to duty on the steamer *Arrow* on July 25 and *Oregon* on July 27. The *Arrow* had been seized by the Governor of Louisiana, armed with a 32-pounder, and turned over to the Confederate army. The larger sidewheel steamer *Oregon* had a brief career as a blockade runner before being similarly seized and armed with one 8-inch gun, a 32-pounder, and two howitzers. These were among the small ships used by the Confederates to control Mississippi Sound and keep open the communications between New Orleans, Ship Island, and Mobile. Commanded by Confederate Navy officers, they also carried Marines and Army personnel to man the guns and form landing parties.[20]

Ship Island was located about ten miles out in the Gulf of Mexico from Biloxi, Mississippi. The Federal government had begun construction of a fort on the island in the late 1850s, which had been seized by Mississippi forces on the secession of that state. The Confederate authorities had recognized the strategic importance of the island, but had dithered throughout the early part of 1861 about what to do with the island and its uncompleted fort. The U.S.S. *Massachusetts* and other Union warships became active in Mississippi Sound and this finally aroused the Confederate authorities to action. Captain Edward Higgins, aide-de-camp to General Twiggs, took command of the *Oregon* and the *Swain*. Higgins had been a lieutenant in the United States Navy before the war and then was commissioned in the 1st Louisiana Heavy Artillery, but his company never completed organization. After stopping at Bay St. Louis, Mississippi, to shield the ships' boilers with cotton bales, the little squadron sailed into the Sound looking for the *Massachusetts*.

They did not find her, but Higgins, realizing the importance of Ship Island, decided on his own initiative to occupy the place. He landed the guns from the ships and a temporary garrison consisting of sailors, fifty-five Confederate Marines under Captain T. T. Thom, and a sergeant and thirty privates of the 4th Louisiana Infantry. Work was immediately begun on sand bag batteries for the 8-inch Columbiad, 32-pounder, and two howitzers. Higgins then returned to New Orleans with the ships and persuaded Twiggs to load the *Oregon* and *Grey Cloud* with guns and ammunition for the island. On July 8, a company of infantry was landed and increased the garrison to seventy-five. They arrived none too soon. That evening the *Massachusetts* anchored to the westward off Chandeleur Island.

As the *Massachusetts* approached Ship Island on July 9, Lieutenant A. F. Warley, C.S. Navy, ordered Midshipman Charles W. Read to open fire with the 8-inch gun, and Midshipman John H. Comstock immediately join-

---

[20] *Official Records of the Union and Confederate Navies in the War of the Rebellion* (Washington: Government Printing Office, 1894-1922), Series I, Vol. XVI, pp. 580-583 (hereafter cited as *NOR*). *Dictionary of American Naval Fighting Ships* (Washington: Naval History Division, 1959-   ), Vol. II, pp. 501, 553.

ed in with the 32-pounder. Both shots fell short. Commodore Melancton Smith of the *Massachusetts* broke out the Stars and Stripes and proceeded to steam within range of the island, replying first with round shot from the bow pivot guns and then coming back and firing 15-second shells with his broadside. His shots too were short. Finally the Confederates managed to lob two shells over the forecastle and engine house which landed uncomfortably close to the *Massachusetts*. Having exhausted his fifteen rounds of 15-second shells, Smith hauled off to a safe distance and hove to until the Confederates ceased firing.

The *Oregon* and the *Grey Cloud* now arrived on the scene from New Orleans. Seeing what was happening, Captain A. L. Myers of the *Oregon* immediately transferred the ammunition supply to the slower *Grey Cloud* and dashed for the island. While the Confederate steamers were anchored at the island unloading supplies, the *Massachusetts* again showed signs of activity. Warley fired four rounds at her and Smith dropped down to Chandeleur Island and anchored. Warley was relieved of command of Ship Island by Lieutenant Colonel Henry W. Allen, 4th Louisiana Infantry. Warley embarked his sailors and Marines on the *Oregon* and set sail for New Orleans.[21]

On the morning of July 13 the *Massachusetts* was back, anchored three miles off Ship Island. The *Oregon* and the *Arrow* got up full steam and headed for the intruder. The *Massachusetts* also got up steam and steadily closed the range. Smith's first shot caused both Confederate vessels to open fire. The *Massachusetts* continued to fire an occasional shot to encourage them, but it soon became apparent that they were trying to lure the larger Federal ship into range of the shore batteries. Smith refused to be lured and the Confederates turned back when he began to get their range. No damage was done by either side.

After their snail-like start, the Confederates were now pouring men and guns onto Ship Island. In July, Twiggs could report he had two heavy shell guns and four 32-pounders mounted on the island with four more heavy guns on the way. Things remained quiet during the month of August. By early September, the garrison of the island consisted of the Washington Light Infantry Company, four companies of the 4th Louisiana Infantry, and Companies B and D of the Confederate regular army recruits, commanded by Second Lieutenant Oliver J. Semmes. In addition there was a small detachment from the Confederate Company of Sappers and Bombardiers of the

---

[21] Richard P. Weinert, "The Neglected Key to The Gulf Coast," *The Journal of Mississippi History*, Vol. XXXI, No. 4 (November 1969), pp. 281-288. Dufour, *Night the War Was Lost*, pp. 48-54. J. Thomas Scharf, *History of the Confederate Navy* (New York: The Fairfax Press, n.d.), pp. 273-274.

regular army commanded by Lieutenant P. N. Judice, assisting Major Martin L. Smith on the construction of the fort, now named Fort Twiggs. Lieutenant Colonel Allen commanded the battalion of the 4th Louisiana Infantry and was the post commander.

On September 3, Colonel Johnson K. Duncan of the 1st Louisiana Heavy Artillery proceeded to Ship Island to take temporary command in the absence of Allen, accompanied by four officers of his regiment to take charge of drilling the heavy gun crews. Duncan had been a lieutenant in the 3d United States Artillery and had been commissioned a captain in the Confederate regular Corps of Artillery. Appointed major of the 1st Louisiana Heavy Artillery, he had been promoted to colonel in July. Duncan was not pleased by much he saw at Ship Island. He found that Fort Twiggs was horseshoe shaped, closed at the gorge with a half-bastion front for land defense. The fort had been designed to have one tier of casemate guns, a tier of barbette guns, and to be surrounded by a moat and glacis. But the construction of the brick walls had progressed only as far as the bottoms of the casemate embrasures. The Confederates had attempted to make the work defensible by completing the brick piers between the embrasures and covering the whole with sand bags. Within the fort more brick piers were being built from which heavy timbers were wedged to brace the outer brick walls, the whole being covered with sand bags and 3-inch planking.

In Duncan's opinion, one shot coming from any direction was bound to hit one of the piers and bring it, the planking, and the sand bags down on the heads of the gunners. The only way the fort could be useful would be to complete it according to the original plans. In its present state a couple of warships could flatten it in short order. Duncan suggested that Fort Twiggs be abandoned entirely and that the only attempt at fortifying the island be a few sand bag batteries along the beach. The most disturbing thing to Duncan was the fact that a shot from the 9-inch Dahlgren gun, the best gun on the island, fell short of Cat Island by a mile and a half. The channel beyond that range still had eighteen feet of water. There were two other channels into the Sound that were not covered at all by the guns on the island. Duncan believed the best protection for the coast from Mobile to the Rigolets was a fleet of shallow draught gunboats.

Although unhappy about most things, Duncan had kind words about the Confederate regulars of Companies B and D.

> The two detachments of regulars are more than sufficient to man all the guns and afford the necessary reliefs. ... The regular detachments there are in command of Lieutenants Semmes and Barnes, from West Point, and as they requested permission to drill their own companies at the heavy guns I of course granted it, these officers being fully competent to the task. These two companies alone can furnish all the necessary reliefs and gun detachments to man and fight the battery at any time.

When Companies B and D were transferred to Ship Island is not known, but they were shown as being present at New Orleans Barracks on the August post return.[22]

Major Martin L. Smith of the Corps of Engineers was one dissenting voice in the cry for abandonment. A captain of Topographical Engineers in the Old Army, Smith had been commissioned a major in the Confederate regular Corps of Engineers. He later became colonel of the 21st Louisiana Infantry and eventually rose to the rank of major general. Smith agreed that work should be pushed on completing the fort according to the original plan and that a gunboat squadron should be provided in the Sound. But he maintained the fort in its present condition would be much better able to withstand an assault than the temporary sand bag emplacements suggested by Duncan. Twiggs forwarded both of these reports to Richmond with the recommendation that the island be abandoned.

On September 13, the War Department ordered Twiggs to immediately evacuate Ship Island and to remove the guns. That afternoon Duncan boarded the *Oregon* and, accompanied by the *Grey Cloud* and the requisitioned civilian steamers *A. G. Brown* and *Ocean Springs,* proceeded to Ship Island, arriving at 1 a.m. on September 14. With a small detail of officers from his regiment and the post garrison, he commenced work on transferring the guns and supplies to the ships. Working through the entire night of September 15, the loading was completed by sundown on September 16. Duncan then set fire to the buildings and lumber on the island and embarked the garrison. He also took the lamp from the lighthouse and burned the stairs. The two regular companies temporarily returned to New Orleans Barracks and Semmes' Company B was detailed to guard prisoners of war in the Parish Prison.[23]

On October 3, the Infantry School battalion was reorganized. Companies A and B were consolidated into a new Company A and Companies C and D were consolidated into a new Company C. Company E remained at Fort Pike. Company A was then attached to a light artillery battery being formed in New Orleans, leaving New Orleans Barracks for its new assignment on October 20. On October 6, under the command of Lieutenant Dixon, Company C had left to join the garrison of Fort Jackson.[24]

---

[22] *OR*, Series I, Vol. VI, pp. 733-734. Post Return, New Orleans Barracks, August 1861, RG 109, NA. Weinert, "Neglected Key", pp. 288-293.

[23] *OR*, Series I, Vol. LIII, pp. 740-741. Special Orders No. 80 and 99, Department No. 1, September 2 and 4, 1861, RG 109, NA. Weinert, "Neglected Key", pp. 293-294. Vincent H. Cassidy and Amos E. Simpson, *Henry Watkins Allen of Louisiana* (Baton Rouge: Louisiana State University Press, 1964), pp. 72-73.

[24] Post Return, New Orleans Barracks, October 1861; Special Order No. 107, Department No. 1, October 4, 1861; RG 109, NA.

Fort Jackson, commanded since 1861 by Colonel Duncan, was located on the right bank of the Mississippi River at Plaquemines Bend sixty-five miles below New Orleans. Built in the 1820's, the brick fort was a regular pentagon with bastions at the angles. An earthen water battery lay outside the main work just down stream and a barrack citadel stood in the center of the fort. Dixon's command originally consisted of 104 officers and men. During November ten men were transferred to the light artillery battery and forty-one recruits were transferred to Company C from New Orleans Barracks.[25]

During December, Company C was assigned to form part of the garrison of Fort St. Philip. Originally built by the Spanish in 1796 and extensively modified by the United States in the 1840's, Fort St. Philip was located about 700 yards higher up the Mississippi and on the opposite bank from Fort Jackson. The fort was an irregular quadrilateral measuring about 150 by 100 yards, and mounting twenty heavy guns bearing on the channel. The external water batteries near the fort mounted fifty-two more guns.[26]

Originally Second Lieutenant Joseph D. Mayes was the only officer besides Dixon with Company C. He was transferred to the light artillery battery on March 22, 1862, and Second Lieutenant Henry L. Blow took his place at Fort St. Philip. Blow had been a lieutenant in the 21st Louisiana Infantry and was commissioned a lieutenant in the regular army in January 1862. On March 10, the 22d Louisiana Infantry was organized from unattached companies at the forts. To complete the regiment, Company C was attached and served as Company K, 22d Louisiana Infantry, but it retained its identity as a regular unit and was mustered separately.[27]

The long awaited attack on the forts began the morning of April 19, when Commander David Dixon Porter's mortar squadron opened fire. The mortar fire was directed exclusively against Fort Jackson. The guns at Fort St. Philip attempted to reply to the Union fire, but were too far upstream to have much effect. On April 22, about 100 men were ordered by Duncan from the garrison of Fort St. Philip to man the guns of the unfinished ironclad *Louisiana.* Most of these apparently were men of Company C under the command of Lieutenant Dixon.[28]

The *Louisiana* was a casemated ironclad roughly similar to the *Merrimack,* only propelled by two side paddles. She had been under construction

[25] Post Return, Forts Jackson and St. Philip, November 1861; Special Order No. 28, Department No. 1, November 18, 1861; RG 109, NA.

[26] Dufour, *Night the War Was Lost,* pp. 220-221.

[27] Post Returns, Forts Jackson and St. Philip, March 1862; Special Order No. 60, Department No. 1, March 22, 1862; General Order No. 8, Department No. 1, March 10, 1862; RG 109, NA. The 22d Louisiana Infantry was subsequently redesignated as the 21st (Patton's) Louisiana Infantry.

[28] *OR,* Series I, Vol. VI, p. 551.

at New Orleans, but when the attack on the fort came her engines were not working and her guns had not been mounted. Over protests of the Navy, the incompleted ironclad was towed down river and tied up to the shore just above Fort St. Philip to act as a floating battery.

In the darkness of early morning on April 24 the Union fleet commanded by Flag Officer David G. Farragut finally began its attempt to run by the forts. The guns at Fort St. Philip fired furiously on the enemy, but some confusion arose in the upper water battery. Captain M. T. Squires, commanding the fort, explained that the guns had originally been manned by Company C which was fully prepared to work the battery, but when they were withdrawn for duty on the *Louisiana* inexperienced men had been detailed to the guns. The *Louisiana* was so poorly designed that its gun ports did not permit the guns to be traversed or elevated and depressed. As the Union fleet steamed by, she fired bravely with 9-inch smoothbores, one 7-inch rifle, one 32-pounder, and two 8-inch smoothbores which bore on the channel. One large Union ship came immediately alongside and fired a broadside into the *Louisiana* which failed to penetrate the armor. The Confederate ship, unable to depress her guns, in turn inflicted little damage. Although her armor shield held, the *Louisiana* took a pounding from the broadsides of the passing fleet and her commander was mortally wounded. There undoubtedly were casualties among the men of Company C, but there is no record of their losses. As Farragut proceeded up the river toward New Orleans, the regulars were returned to Fort St. Philip that evening. By then it was too late.[29]

After the Union fleet had passed the forts the Confederate garrisons were hopelessly cut off. Dixon accompanied Captain Squires to a conference at Fort Jackson on April 28. They reported that under the circumstances there was no choice but to surrender. Casualties in the forts during the engagement were surprisingly light, but a mutiny by most of the garrison of Fort Jackson on April 27 made further resistance hopeless. The troops at Fort St. Philip had not yet mutinied, but Squires felt that, considering conditions at Fort Jackson, his men could not be trusted. Duncan swallowed his humiliation and surrendered the forts to Porter.[30]

The behavior of Company C following the surrender was disgraceful, but not unique. New Orleans was the most cosmopolitan city of the South. A large proportion of the militia and the few volunteer units which defended the city were composed of soldiers of foreign birth. There had been trouble

[29] *Ibid.*, pp. 551-552; *ORN.* Series I, Vol. XVIII, p. 292; Scharf, *Confederate Navy*, pp. 281-301.

[30] *OR*, Series I, Vol. VI, pp. 531-532.

with these troops in February, when it was rumored that they would be sent into Confederate service outside the city. These units willingly fought to defend New Orleans, but once the city had fallen they no longer felt any attachment to the cause of the Confederacy. The regular troops of the Infantry School of Practice were little different from these Louisiana units. Although they had been recruited from a much larger geographical area, the percentage of foreign born was very high. Available records show that 47.2 percent of the Infantry School recruits were foreign born. Actually the figure was probably well over 50 percent, but the lack of enlistment papers for all recruits makes it impossible to give an exact figure.[31]

General Duncan summed up the situation following the fall of the city when he wrote from New Orleans on May 13:

> I endeavored, the best of my ability, to see that they (the garrisons) were properly cared for until such time as they could be sent out of town. … Not withstanding that they were amply provided for, scores of them have been daily going over to the enemy and enlisting since, until now there are but a very few left from either fort not in the ranks of the enemy. Although I really did think at the time of the surrender that some few of the men were loyal, the facts which have since come to light have perfectly satisfied me that nearly every man in both forts was thoroughly implicated and concerned in the revolt on the night of April 27.[32]

With the exception of the men in the light artillery battery, only ten other men of the Infantry School who were in New Orleans or at the forts ever rejoined the Confederate Army. Privates James Finn and Frederick Greves had been serving on detached duty as orderlies at Department Headquarters and with Brigadier General Martin L. Smith, respectively. Sergeant Cornelius O'Leary had been on extra duty in the Quartermaster Department with Captain Edward Powell. These three men went with Department Headquarters when it retreated to Jackson, Mississippi. It is interesting to note that Greves is found as late as November 30, 1863, in Athens, Georgia, serving on detached service from Company C, C.S. Recruits.[33]

Private Frederick Heine is the only regular from the forts found to have rejoined the Confederates. After the surrender he was taken to New Orleans and paroled. He reported for duty in May and was serving in Jackson, in June. Still being on parole, he was sent to Camp Lee, Virginia until exchanged. After his exchange he became first sergeant of Company B, Camp Lee Guard. On June 2, 1864, Heine requested his discharge since his enlistment

---

[31] For the attitude of the foreign troops in and around New Orleans, see Dufour, *Night the War Was Lost*, pp. 181-184. The figures for the Infantry School of Practice were computed from information in the *CMSR*, Infantry School of Practice, and enlistment papers in the "Unfileable File," RG 109, NA.

[32] *OR*, Series I, Vol. VI, p. 535.

[33] *CMSR*, Infantry School of Practice; vouchers, enlistment papers in "Unfileable File;" and Receipt Roll No. 204; RG 109, NA.

was up. This caused some confusion at headquarters, but it was finally determined that he had enlisted for three years as a regular and not being a citizen could not be held in service. Sergeant Heine was discharged on August 26, 1864, probably the last man of Company C still in service.[34]

A total of 254 men served with Company C at one time or another, and nine of these were former United States regulars. Existing records show 56 deserted, 7 died, 10 were discharged, there is no final record for 58, 107 were probably captured at Fort St. Philip and there is no later record, 10 rejoined the Confederates, and there is no record after enlistment of 6. Nine of the men have been found to have later joined the Union army, most of these in the 9th Connecticut Infantry, but the number is probably much higher. Edmond Downing had been a sergeant in the 3d United States Infantry, and had been discharged in 1854. He enlisted in New Orleans in 1861 and became a sergeant in Company C. Following his capture he enlisted in May 1862 in the 9th Connecticut Infantry and was mustered out in 1865 as a second lieutenant.

Company E had been at Fort Pike since July 1861. On July 13, 1861, Second Lieutenant Lucius D. Sandidge was assigned to command the company, being succeeded on August 15 by Second Lieutenant George H. Frost. Both had been cadets at West Point when they resigned and were commissioned in the Confederate regular Corps of Artillery. On January 1, 1862, seventy-six men of Company E were assigned to form Company I, 1st Louisiana Heavy Artillery, and eight men were attached to Company H of that regiment at Fort Jackson and were subsequently captured on April 27. Lieutenant Frost and a detachment of fifteen regulars remained at Fort Pike. On March 2, this detachment was broken up, the men being attached to Companies A and I, 1st Louisiana Heavy Artillery.[35]

On March 20, two regulars from Company A and three from Company I were placed on detached service on the C.S.S. *Carondelet*. This light draft steamer had been built by the Confederates and was armed with five 42-pounders and a 32-pounder. On April 4, accompanied by the *Oregon* and the *Pamlico,* she engaged three Federal gunboats at Pass Christian, Mississippi, but was unable to prevent the landing of 1,200 Union troops and the destruction of the Confederate camp there. With the fall of the forts on the Mississippi, the *Carondelet* was destroyed on Lake Ponchartrain and Fort Pike was abandoned, being reoccupied by Federal forces on April 27. During the retreat of the garrison to Camp Moore, near Kentwood, Louisiana,

---

[34] Heine to Maj. T. G. Peyton, June 2, 1864, *CMSR,* Conscripts, Camp Lee, Va.; Special Order No. 202, A&IGO, August 26, 1864; RG 109, NA. Heine was a German.

[35] Post Returns, Fort Pike, July 1861, August 1861, January 1862, and March 1862; Special Order No. 45, Department No. 1, February 27, 1862; RG 109, NA.

one regular of Company A and nineteen of Company I deserted.[36]

The 1st Louisiana Heavy Artillery did not remain long at Camp Moore, arriving in Vicksburg during May. Brigadier General Martin L. Smith assumed command of the defenses of Vicksburg on May 12 and frantically rushed completion of the batteries defending the city. The first of Farragut's ships had proceeded up the river after the fall of New Orleans and captured Baton Rouge without resistance. On May 18, they arrived at Vicksburg and demanded its surrender, which Smith promptly refused. The Federal fleet began the bombardment of the city of May 26 and until the middle of June firing of more or less heavy intensity continued. With the arrival of the mortar ships from New Orleans on June 26, Farragut was ready for his main attack. In a fierce battle on June 28, the Federal fleet managed to fight its way past the Confederate batteries. They did not manage to silence a single Confederate gun. One regular of Company A was wounded in the attack. Bombardment of the city continued, one regular of Company I being killed on July 3 and another dying of wounds the following day.[37]

Major General Earl Van Dorn had been ordered to assume command of Vicksburg on June 20. With Van Dorn, Company A, 1st Confederate Regular Cavalry, arrived in Vicksburg. Soon after Van Dorn and Company A departed the city in September, two men of Company I, 1st Louisiana Heavy Artillery, were transferred to Company A of the cavalry. The two companies of the 1st Louisiana Heavy Artillery, kept up to reasonable strength with Louisiana conscripts, remained at Vicksburg and participated in the memorable siege until the Confederate surrender on July 4, 1863. Besides the dangers of combat, the year in Vicksburg had taken a heavy toll as eight men of Company I died of disease. Following the surrender, fifteen men deserted or refused to be paroled and spent the remainder of the war as prisoners of war. Following his parole after the capture of Vicksburg, Frost, promoted to temporary captain in the regulars, served as assistant inspector general on Brigadier General Frank C. Armstrong's staff and so continued his association with regular units.

On September 7, 1863, Major General Dabney Maury requested that the 1st Louisiana Heavy Artillery be sent to Mobile as soon as it was exchanged. On that date, the remnants of the regiment were camped at Enterprise, Mississippi, as paroled prisoners of war. The regiment was finally exchanged on January 1, 1864, and on January 13 it was ordered to Mobile and became part of Colonel Charles A. Fuller's Artillery Brigade of the

---

[36] *Naval Fighting Ships*, Vol. II, p. 506.

[37] *OR*, Series I, Vol. XV, pp. 6-9. A. T. Mahan, *The Gulf and Inland Waters* (New York: The Blue & Gray Press, n.d.), pp. 90-97.

District of the Gulf. The regiment apparently was ordered away from Mobile in the summer of 1864 as when the Federals attacked Fort Gaines in Mobile Bay on August 4, Maury requested General Bragg to return it to Mobile. In early 1865, the regiment was serving as part of the Artillery Reserve of the left wing of the defenses of Mobile. When Mobile fell on April 12, four more men of Company I deserted. With the surrender of Lieutenant General Richard Taylor's forces, nine remaining regulars of Company I and two of Company A were paroled at Meridian, Mississippi, on May 14. The two men of Company A were both former United States regulars.[38]

In four hard years of service, ninety regulars served with Company E, Infantry School of Practice, and subsequently with Companies A and I, 1st Louisiana Heavy Artillery. Of these, 2 were killed in action or died of wounds, 2 died while prisoners of war, 9 died of disease or other causes, 7 were discharged, 3 were transferred, 53 deserted, there is no final record for 2, and 10 were paroled at the end of the war. Four of the men had previous United States regular army service, three deserters joined the Union army, and one had subsequent Confederate service. Six of the men who refused to be paroled after the surrender of Vicksburg became prisoners of war.

Company A and B, Infantry School of Practice, had been consolidated into Company A on October 3, 1861, at New Orleans Barracks. This company was attached to a light artillery battery on October 16.[39] Captain Edward Higgins, 1st Louisiana Heavy Artillery, had been ordered to organize a light artillery battery on October 9.[40] Higgins' efforts to organize the battery in the last months of 1861 were successful, but apparently he resigned his army commission in January 1862 to organize a navy for the state of Louisiana. The plan was foiled by the Confederate Navy and Army and in February he became lieutenant colonel of the 1st Louisiana Heavy Artillery and commanded Fort Jackson during Farragut's attack.[41]

Oliver Semmes was the son of Confederate naval hero Captain Raphael Semmes and had been a cadet at West Point when the war started. Semmes apparently remained with the regular recruits from the time they were attached to Higgins' command. He was joined on October 17 by Second Lieutenant John T. Mason Barnes, who had served with him on Ship Island. The company was mustered on October 29 with 120 rank and file. It had left

---

[38] *OR*, Series I, Vol. XVII, Part 2, p. 661; Vol. XXIV, Part 3, pp. 615, 704; Vol. XXX, Part 4, p. 620; Vol. XXXI, Part 3, p. 727; Vol. XXXII, Part 2, pp. 506, 553, and Part 3, p. 861; Vol. XLIX, Part 1, p. 1047; Vol. LII, Part 2, pp. 718, 719. Parole Roll No. 83. Meridian, Miss., RG 109, NA.

[39] Special Order No. 118, Department No. 1, October 16, 1861, RG 109, NA.

[40] Special Order No. 112, Department No. 1, October 9, 1861, RG 109, NA.

[41] Hamersly, *General Navy Register*, p. 345, Dufour, *Night the War Was Lost*, p. 169. *CMSR*, Lt. Col. Edward Higgins, 1st Louisiana Heavy Artillery, RG 109, NA.

New Orleans Barracks on October 20, apparently being stationed at Camp Lewis, about one and a half miles below Carrollton and just above New Orleans. The drummers with the company were transferred to Company E on November 4 and by the end of that month the aggregate company strength was about 115.[42]

With the resignation of Higgins, Semmes apparently became commander of the battery, although he was not promoted to the temporary regular rank of captain until March 3, 1862.[43] One of the major problems facing Major General Mansfield Lovell, who had succeeded Twiggs in command of Department No. 1, was the con-

MAJOR OLIVER J. SEMMES
Courtesy of Museum of The City of Mobile

stant calls made on him from other fronts for troops. On February 20, Brigadier General Daniel Ruggles at Corinth requested that Semmes' battery be sent to him. Lovell apparently was able to ignore this request since the light artillery battery was reported in New Orleans when the Union Navy arrived.[44] With the evacuation of New Orleans the battery, which by now was designated the 1st Confederate Regular Light Artillery Battery, moved to Camp Moore and was assigned to the First Sub-District of Van Dorn's District of the Mississippi.

---

[42] Special Order No. 119, Department No. 1, October 17, 1861; Special Order No. 10, Department No. 1, October 29, 1861; Special Order No. 12, Department No. 1, November 4, 1861; Quartermaster Receipts, dated New Orleans Barracks, November 13 and 22, 1861, in *CMSR*, Lt. Col. Edward Higgins, Staff File; RG 109, NA. Thomas W. Owen, *History of Alabama and Dictionary of Alabama Biography* (Chicago: S. J. Clarke Publishing Co., 1921), Vol. IV, pp. 1525-1526. Powell A. Casey, *Encyclopedia of Forts, Posts, Named Camps, and Other Military Installations In Louisiana, 1700-1981* (Baton Rouge: Claitor's Publishing Division, 1983), pp. 104-105. Arthur W. Bergeron, Jr., *Guide to Louisiana Confederate Military Units, 1861-1865* (Baton Rouge: Louisiana State University Press, 1989), pp. 18-19. Semmes says in "First Confederate Battery An Orphan," *Confederate Veteran*, Vol. XXI (1913), p. 58, that the men were mostly Irish and German and nearly all had been soldiers in the United States Army. This cannot be documented.

[43] *CMSR*, Maj. O. J. Semmes, Staff File, RG 109, NA.

[44] *OR*, Series I, Vol. VI, p. 620, and Vol. VII, pp. 894-895. The company muster roll, dated April 30, 1862, at Camp Moore, states that it moved from Camp Lewis on April 21 and arrived at Camp Moore on April 22, under orders from Brig. Gen. M. L. Smith; RG 109, NA.

The 1st Confederate Light Artillery Battery was soon to see its first action. Major General John C. Breckinridge's division reached Camp Moore from Vicksburg on July 28. Here it joined a small force under General Ruggles and was divided into two divisions for the advance on Baton Rouge, which was held by a Union force under Brigadier General Thomas Williams. In this expedition the 1st Regular Battery was attached to the Second Brigade of Ruggles' Second Division.

The evening of August 4 a section of the 1st Regular Battery commanded by Second Lieutenant Thomas K. Fauntleroy was detached with three companies to advance on Baton Rouge down the Clunton Road. Fauntleroy had begun the war as a private in the 6th Virginia Cavalry before being commissioned in the regular army in July. As the first scattered shots of the main advance began, Fauntleroy's section advanced under the command of Lieutenant Colonel Thomas Shields against the enemy right flank. The section was posted so that it raked the 14th Maine Infantry and allowed the Confederates to advance within 250 yards of the enemy camp. The Federals were soon reenforced and the small Confederate force began to pull back. Four of the artillery horses were killed, and Sergeant Philip Bellam was seriously wounded, but the horses were quickly replaced and the guns safely withdrawn to join the main Confederate body. Shields had warm praise for Fauntleroy and the regulars, but felt they could have done much better service except for faulty friction primers, nine out of ten of which proved worthless.

Fog shrouded the woods and fields around Baton Rouge the morning of August 5 as Semmes and the main section of the 1st Regulars went into position between Colonel H. W. Allen's and Colonel A. P. Thompson's brigades. The Confederates advance struck the 21st Indiana Infantry, which was supported by the 6th Massachusetts Battery. A well directed fire by the 1st Regulars and Ruggles' infantry soon forced the withdrawal of the Union battery and infantry. Semmes was then shifted to the right flank of the division to cover the advance and continue to engage the 6th Massachusetts. Semmes' gunners also poured grape and canister into an attempt at a Union counterattack, breaking up the advancing column.

The Confederates had captured two of the enemy's camps, but by this time, both brigade commanders of the Second Division and the commander of the First Division were badly wounded and the lines were in great confusion. General Williams had decided to pull back the Union troops under the cover of the gunboats in the river, but, just as this movement began, he was killed. Breckinridge had also had enough, and leaving Semmes with a section of guns supported by the 7th Kentucky Infantry, the Confederates also withdrew. The rear guard held the enemy in check while the stragglers and wounded were gathered up. The weary troops camped on the battlefield, but when it was learned that the powerful ironclad *Arkansas* was unable to reach Baton Rouge to drive off the gunboats, Breckinridge decided to retreat.

The 1st Regulars had a bloody baptism of fire. Five men had been killed, five seriously wounded, and five slightly wounded. Nine horses were killed, two badly wounded, two missing, one caisson blown up by an enemy shell, and another smashed so badly it was abandoned. Semmes fired 200 rounds of smoothbore 6-pounder ammunition and 120 rounds of 6-pounder rifled ammunition during the battle.[45]

The 1st Regulars went into camp near Port Hudson, which Breckinridge began to fortify.[46] The campaign had at least accomplished one thing — the Union army evacuated Baton Rouge on August 21. Breckinridge felt Port Hudson was a much stronger position and did not attempt to occupy the capital city. On August 30, while at Port Hudson, the battery, supported by the 30th Louisiana Infantry, fired four rounds at the Union gunboat *Anglo-American,* causing some casualties. The 1st Regulars did not remain long at Port Hudson. On September 2, they were ordered to cross the Mississippi and report to Major General Richard Taylor at Opelousas, Louisiana. The battery had seen its last service east of the Mississippi.[47]

Semmes joined Colonel W. C. Vincent's small command at Donaldsonville, where Bayou La Fourche leaves the Mississippi above New Orleans. Vincent had made good use of his small force, harassing Union ships on the Mississippi and gathering supplies from the surrounding country for the Confederates. To clear the area, Colonel James A. McMillan and the 21st Indiana Infantry, accompanied by three gunboats, on September 22 easily captured Donaldsonville and drove the Confederates four miles down the La Fourche. On September 22, McMillan advanced his regiment, accompanied by a small artillery battery, to the vicinity of Cox's Plantation. Here the Union force encountered the 1st Regulars, which provided more opposition than they had bargained for. The advance halted and before McMillan could organize an attack on Semmes' battery Confederate cavalry appeared on the flank and rear of the Union troops. McMillan broke off the engagement, beating a hasty retreat back to Donaldsonville. Despite all the shooting,

---

[45] Report of Semmes, August 8, 1862, *OR,* Series I, Vol. XV, pp. 107-108. This is the only battle report of Semmes found for the entire war and is very sketchy. The story of the 1st Regulars in this action has been pieced together from other reports in the cited volume on pp. 78-79, 82, 84, 90-93, 99, 100, 102, 105-106. The report of Col. N.A.M. Dudley, 30th Massachusetts Infantry, p. 60, refers to "Semmes' celebrated battery."

[46] Muster Roll, 1st Confederate Regular Light Artillery Battery, August 31, 1862, Camp near Port Hudson, La., RG 109, NA. This is the last battery muster roll on file. Abstract of Morning Report of Troops at Port Hudson, La., August 31, 1862, *OR,* Series 1, Vol. XV, p. 804, shows an aggregate battery strength of 103.

[47] Special Order No. 58, Army of the Mississippi, September 2, 1862, *OR,* Series I, Vol., XVII, Part 2, p. 691. Richard Taylor, *Destruction and Reconstruction* (New York: Longmans, Green and Co., 1955), p. 133. Alwyn Barr, "Confederate Artillery in Western Louisiana, 1862-1863," *Civil War History,* IX (May 1963), pp. 74-75. Muster Roll, Company C, 30th Louisiana Infantry, August 30, 1862, RG 109, NA.

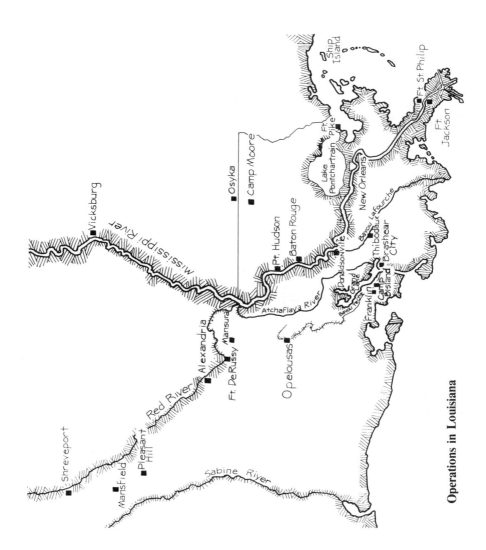

Operations in Louisiana

apparently the only casualty on either side was Lieutenant George C. Harding of the Indiana regiment, who was cut off and captured during the confusion before the retreat. Harding later wrote:

> I also met Capt. Semmes and Lieut. Fauntleroy, of the battery. Semmes was a slight, sallow-faced, volatile man, apparently not more than twenty-one years old, a son of 'Sumter' Semmes, the commander of the Alabama. I felt a good deal of curiosity to see him as we were already acquainted with his battery — having had the benefit of a formal introduction at Baton Rouge. Fauntleroy was a fine-looking, amiable, red-headed young fellow, with the most amusing 'shutter' in conversation.[48]

A Union expedition under Brigadier General Godfrey Weitzel forced Vincent to fall back from the La Fourche and he was joined by Brigadier General Alfred Mouton's command. On October 27, the Union forces caught up with Mouton at Georgia Landing just north of Labadieville. After a sharp fight, during which the 1st Regulars were engaged on the left bank of the bayou, Mouton was driven back and decided to evacuate the La Fourche district. The Federals lost 18 killed and 74 wounded and the Confederates 5 killed, 8 wounded, and 186 captured, most of the latter during the retreat.[49] The 1st Regulars moved by train to Berwick Bay, which they crossed and took up position on Bayou Teche.

About fourteen miles above Brashear City the Confederates placed obstructions in the bayou protected by the gunboat *A. J. Cotton,* the Pelican Light Artillery, and a section of the 1st Regulars commanded by Second Lieutenant John A. A. West. On November 3, the Union gunboats *Calhoun, Colonel Kinsman, Diana,* and *Estrella* advanced up the bayou and engaged the Confederates near Cornay's residence on the right bank. The two bronze 12-pounder rifles of the 1st Regulars, two 3-inch Parrott rifles of the Pelican Artillery, and four guns of the *Cotton* pounded the gunboats for about thirty minutes before falling back along the Bayou Teche road. The Confederates soon stopped and engaged the enemy for another fifteen minutes before withdrawing to Camp Bisland, midway between Brashear City and Franklin. The *Kinsman* was hit 54 times, having one killed and five wounded. The *Estrella,* while hit only three times, lost two killed and one badly wounded. The *Diana* had her stern shot away by three shells and the *Calhoun* was hit eight times. The Confederates, who had hidden among the live oaks, suffered no casualties. The badly mauled Union flotilla withdrew to Brashear City to lick its wounds.[50]

---

[48] *OR,* Series I, Vol. XV, pp. 141-142; George C. Harding, *The Miscellaneous Writings of George C. Harding* (Indianapolis: Carlon & Hollenbeck, 1882), pp. 317-322.

[49] *OR,* Series I, Vol. XV, pp. 168, 172, 176, 178. Taylor, *Destruction and Reconstruction,* p.134.

[50] *OR,* Series I, Vol. XV, pp. 183-185, 1087; *Naval Fighting Ships,* Vol. II, pp. 12, 144, 275, 370, 536.

Two events in March 1863 resulted in significant changes in the Confederate war effort in Louisiana. On March 7, Lieutenant General Edmund Kirby Smith replaced Lieutenant General Theophilus Holmes as commander of the Trans-Mississippi Department. Taylor retained command of the District of Louisiana, but Kirby Smith took a much more direct role in that state than Holmes ever had. Also in early March a brigade of Texas cavalry, which had participated in the New Mexico Campaign and was now commanded by Colonel Thomas Green, arrived and was sent by Taylor to Camp Bisland.[51]

The 1st Regulars remained at Camp Bisland on Bayou Teche, with one section sometimes stationed at Cote Blanche on the Gulf coast until April 1863. On April 9, two divisions of the Nineteenth Corps and Weitzel's Brigade crossed Berwick Bay and began a campaign to clear Bayou Teche of Confederates. The 1st Regulars advanced from their camp to a line of entrenchments covering the bayou which was called Fort Bisland by the Union troops. The four smoothbore 6-pounders under Lieutenants Barnes and Fauntleroy were placed on the left of the line west of the bayou while two 3-inch rifles under Lieutenant West went into position midway between the bayou and a swamp on the extreme right. Throughout the day the 1st Regulars fired on the enemy but it was not until just before the Union attack that Semmes and many of his men were detached on the gunboat *Diana,* which had been captured by the Confederates on March 20 during a reconnaissance on Grand Lake and the Atchafalaya. Semmes hotly contested the enemy advance until a 30-pounder Parrott shell from the 18th New York Battery penetrated the plating in front of the boilers and exploded in the engine room, killed two and wounding five of the gunboat's crews. The *Diana* then withdrew from the action for repairs. During this time the 1st Regulars, under the command of Lieutenant Barnes, continued to keep up a steady fire. The section under Lieutenant West was several times sent to join the forces covering the rear, but each time was returned to the line before it had gone far. The enemy attack was repulsed, but that night Taylor learned that Brigadier General Cuvier Grover's division had landed in his rear.[52]

Taylor began an immediate withdrawal. West's section was detached to cover the retreat, displacing from point to point until it reached Centerville. Here he masked the pieces and covered by Colonel Thomas Green's 5th Texas Cavalry fired into the advancing Union column at close range. He then opened an effective fire on a bunched up battery, but by this time a second battery had arrived and the Union infantry was deploying. West and Green then fought a retiring action, stopping every 500 yards to fire on

[51] Taylor, *Destruction and Reconstruction,* pp. 149-150; Joseph H. Parks, *General E. Kirby Smith, C.S.A.* (Baton Rouge: Louisiana State University Press, 1954), p. 253.

[52] *OR,* Series I, Vol. XV, pp. 680, 390. and Vol. LIII, p. 463; Taylor, *Destruction and Reconstruction,* pp. 153-154; Barr, "The Confederate Artillery in Western Louisiana," p. 79.

the enemy until they covered the five miles to Franklin. West then covered the burning of the bridge two miles from Franklin and a second bridge several more miles up the bayou. He reached Jeanerette that night without losing a man or a gun.[53]

At first light on April 14, Taylor's troops struck Grover's surprised division at Irish Bend near Franklin. The road was cleared, but a fierce fight followed. Suddenly the peculiar sound of a Parrott shell announced the arrival of Semmes and the *Diana*. Under the heavy covering fire Taylor managed to get his men past the position. Just after Taylor got clear, Green and West arrived, still holding back the advance of Brigadier General William H. Emory's Federal division. Semmes kept the *Diana* in position and covered the successful withdrawal of the rear guard. He then abandoned the gunboat and blew it up. By this time the enemy had arrived in full force and Semmes and his crew were captured before they could get away.[54]

The Confederate retreat continued, with Fauntleroy and a section of guns relieving West's section with Green on April 15. Fauntleroy engaged Battery F, 1st United States Artillery, at Jeanerette, but was soon forced to withdraw before the superior numbers of the enemy. Barnes commanded a section on picket duty near Opelousas on April 18 and then retreated to Lecompte near the Red River. During the campaign the 1st Regulars had lost 1 man killed, 2 wounded, 25 missing, and 1 caisson destroyed. Many of the missing were captured although quite a few apparently deserted during the retreat.[55]

Semmes and the other officers captured during the campaign were placed on the *Maple Leaf,* an Army transport, which sailed from New Orleans for New York on June 2. The ship was diverted to Fort Monroe on June 8, where it picked up more prisoners and then headed for Fort Delaware. Off Cape Henry, at the mouth of Chesapeake Bay, on June 10, the prisoners captured the ship and twenty-four, including Semmes, made good their escape. The fugitives made their way to North Carolina and eluded Union cavalry which had been dispatched to recapture them near Elizabeth City. By September, Semmes had managed to recross the Mississippi despite threats to hang him if captured, and again took command of the 1st Regulars.[56]

Taylor's small force was not strong enough to hold permanently all of western Louisiana, but he kept the Union troops under constant pressure. In early June, Taylor determined that the Union garrison at Brashear City

---

[53] *OR,* Series I, Vol. XV, p. 392, and Vol. LIII, pp. 464-465, 469.

[54] *OR,* Series I, Vol. XV, pp. 392, 395, and Vol. LIII, pp. 463-464; Taylor, *Destruction and Reconstruction,* pp. 158-159.

[55] *OR,* Series I, Vol. LIII, p. 464.

[56] *OR,* Series I, Vol. XXVII, Part 2, p. 786, and Part 3, pp. 206, 901; and Series II, Vol. VI, pp. 70-71, 90.

on Berwick Bay was vulnerable and launched a two-pronged drive. Green had been promote to brigadier general in May and given command of the Texas cavalry brigade. The capture of Brashear City was assigned to Mouton, whose forces had reoccupied Camp Bisland, while Colonel James P. Major's Brigade aimed at the railroad crossing of the La Fourche to cut off the Union retreat. Major's command was at Washington, above Opelousas. Taylor gave Major minute instructions and guides and ordered him to follow the Grosse Tete to Plaquemine on the Mississippi and then take the road that reached the La Fourche some distance below Donaldsonville.

Major's command, including the 1st Regulars, crossed the Atchafalaya on June 12. Finding the bridge across Bayou Sara burned, the Confederate force marched to Waterloo. Here they spent the day of June 15 demonstrating against a Union force from Port Hudson. That night Major's command moved to Bayou Grosse Tete and marching down that stream captured Plaquemine on June 18. The Confederates then marched down the shore of the Mississippi River, managing to avoid being seen by three Union gunboats. Arriving at Bayou Goula, Major's troops captured commissary and quartermaster stores, destroyed the Federal plantations, and recaptured over 1,000 Negroes. Deciding that Donaldsonville was too strongly fortified to be attacked, Major feinted toward the town and then moved his command in two sections toward Thibodeaux.

Finding the road blocked by the Federals and impracticable for artillery, Major sent Lieutenant West of the 1st Regulars with a party of Negroes to clear an alternate route and on June 20 the entire column was able to advance. Meanwhile, Colonel W. P. Lane's 1st Texas Partisan Cavalry, which had gone ahead of the main column, captured Pancourtville and Terre Bonne Station, taking a large number of prisoners and supplies.

Major reached Thibodeaux on the afternoon of June 21. The next morning, pickets reported Union reenforcements advancing from New Orleans. The 1st Regulars, Pyron's 2d Texas Cavalry, and two other cavalry squadrons were posted on the east bank of the La Fourche and moved toward the railroad bridge while three regiments moved from Terre Bonne Station to La Fourche Crossing. The Federals then fell back and a heavy rain stopped any Confederate pursuit. Major's troops were short of ammunition and the rain ruined most of what was left. Pyron, as soon as it stopped raining, attacked the enemy position and captured four guns and many prisoners. The arrival of fresh Federal reenforcements that night forced Pyron to fall back and the following day Major marched toward Brashear City, covered by his artillery.

Arriving at Chacachoula Station just before dawn on June 23, the Confederates were delighted to hear the sound of artillery fire at Brashear City. This was the first they had heard of Mouton's column since the expedition started. Driving in the Federal pickets, Major's column arrived at Bayou Boeuf that afternoon. Major crossed the bayou the following morning and prepared to attack the enemy force. Before he could open fire with his artillery, a white flag appeared. The enemy had already surrendered to Mouton, whose force was five miles away. Thus ended one of the most impressive small campaigns of the war. Two columns starting more than a hundred miles apart managed to converge almost exactly on time and defeat an unsuspecting enemy. Mouton's force captured at Brashear City over 1,700 prisoners, twelve heavy guns, and a vast quantity of quartermaster, commissary, and ordnance stores. Major on his way to join Mouton burned two steamers and captured four guns and 100 prisoners. Capture of a train trying to escape from Berwick Bay enabled the Confederates to operate the line as far east as La Fourche.[57]

On June 24, Green led his and Major's brigades, including the 1st Regulars, toward Donaldsonville. Green deployed his troops around Fort Butler at that town on the night of June 27 and launched a furious assault the following morning. Storming the palisade, the attacking party was trapped in the ditch inside the work and suffered heavy casualties before Green could break off the engagement and retreat. During the withdrawal down the La Fourche, the 1st Regulars and the 4th Texas Cavalry on June 30 badly damaged the Federal transport *Iberville* at College Point and the following day a section of the battery engaged the enemy flagship *Monongahela*.[58]

After again serving on Bayou Teche, the battery accompanied Green's Brigade and two brigades of infantry in an advance across the Atchafalaya against the Union outpost at Sterling's Plantation on Bayou Fordouche near Morganza. West's section of the 1st Regulars deployed with the 4th and 5th Texas Cavalry and fired on the enemy cavalry near the Catlett house. Meanwhile the other two sections of the battery with the 7th Texas Cavalry pushed rapidly down the road toward Fordouche Bridge. The battery was reunited at the bridge and the cavalry charged and routed the enemy. When the firing ceased, Green had captured two entire Union regiments, two guns, and much equipment and had routed the rest of the enemy force. After a demonstration toward Morganza, Green returned with his force to Opelousas and then joined Mouton.[59]

On November 7, with the warm endorsement of Major Thomas L. Brent, Taylor's chief of artillery, Semmes was promoted to major in the Provisional

[57] *OR*, Series I, Vol. XXVI, Part 1, pp. 217-219; Taylor, *Destruction and Reconstruction*, pp. 167-171.

[58] *OR*, Series I, Vol. XXVI, Part 1, pp. 216, 227-228, 615; Taylor, *Destruction and Reconstruction*, pp. 171-172.

[59] *OR*, Series I, Vol. XXVI, Part 1, pp. 662, 329-330, 323, and Part 2, p. 295; Taylor, *Destruction and Reconstruction*, pp. 179-180.

Army and given command of a battalion. Barnes in turn was promoted to captain in the Provisional Army and assumed command of the 1st Regulars.[60] On December 19, from surplus captured guns, Taylor organized the 6th Louisiana Battery and promoted West to captain in the Provisional Army to take command. Although this battery was formed with surplus guns belonging to the 1st Regulars, West was apparently the only member of the regulars transferred to the new battery. Semmes served as Green's chief of artillery and the 1st Regulars were placed under Major Thomas A. Faries, the chief of artillery of Major General John A. Wharton's Second Infantry Division.[61]

The 1st Regulars were probably with Green's cavalry division near the Texas coast in early 1864 when Major General N. P. Banks began his Red River Campaign. This campaign had been launched by Banks and Rear Admiral David D. Porter in an attempt to secure most of Louisiana and East Texas. The expedition was also expected to secure large quantities of cotton and it was hoped that it might help deter French ambitions in Mexico. In addition to the main military and naval force move up the Red River, a supporting Union column also began to advance from Arkansas. Green's troops finally reached Taylor's army in western Louisiana during the first week of April and participated in the defeat of the Union expedition on April 8 and 9 at Mansfield and Pleasant Hill. Mouton was killed leading a charge at Mansfield. On April 11, the 1st Regulars were attached to Colonel Arthur P. Bagby's cavalry brigade, which had returned to Mansfield from Pleasant Hill, and ordered to Grand Bayou. Before reaching the ferry over Bayou Pierre, Bagby found that Union cavalry had managed to warn the Federal fleet, which turned back down the Red River from Boggy Bayou. After a delay in crossing Bayou Pierre by ferry, he missed catching up with the Union fleet. Bagby continued down the river, reaching Blair's Landing on the evening of April 12. Green and the 6th Louisiana Battery had caught up with the enemy earlier that day at Blair's Landing. The Union transports were subjected to a punishing fire, but Green was killed in the engagement.

Major, who had been promoted to brigadier general in June 1863, took command of the cavalry gathered near Blair's Landing and returned to Pleasant Hill and then joined the Confederate forces that had moved to Grand Ecore and Natchitoches. The 1st Regulars along with Colonel William H. Parson's Texas cavalry brigade began to pursue the enemy down the Red River on April 22. On April 23, Parson's Brigade caught up with the enemy near Cloutierville and came under artillery fire. Barnes arrived with three

---

[60] Maj. J. L. Brent to Taylor, September 8, 1863, in *CMSR*, Maj. O. J. Semmes, Staff File, RG 109, NA.

[61] *CMSR*, Capt. John A. A. West, 6th Louisiana Battery and Staff File, RG 109, NA. West was promoted to major in August 1864 and served later in the war as Taylor's chief of artillery in the Department of Alabama, Mississippi, and East Louisiana.

of his guns during the engagement and effectively replied to the enemy fire. That night Barnes shelled the Union camp four miles below Cloutierville producing confusion and consternation. A sharp action took place the following day and the Confederates were at first forced back. Barnes, however, shelled the Union column, which broke in confusion bringing an end to the battle. Barnes' 12-pounders were again brought up on April 27 to fire on a Union gunboat as the enemy withdrew into Alexandria. On the night of May 4-5, Major with West's battery attacked two gunboats and a transport near Fort DeRussy, some fifteen miles below Alexandria. A gunboat was blown up to avoid capture and two other ships fell into Confederate hands. Barnes then moved into position with his heavier guns near Fort DeRussy in an attempt to block the Federal escape from Alexandria and to prevent reenforcements.[62]

The last of the Federal forces managed to get by the falls of the Red River at Alexandria and evacuated the town on May 13. Wharton's Second Infantry Division, with the 1st Regulars now part of Faries' battalion, took position on May 15 on the prairie one and a quarter miles south of Mansura. Here on the morning of May 16 they encountered the rear of Banks' retreating forces, composed of elements of the Nineteenth Corps. Two 30-pounder Parrotts were positioned at the entrance to the road running parallel to the Long Bridge road, with Cornay's Louisiana battery on the right 600 yards in front of the Parrotts and the 1st Regulars on the left in advance of the big rifles.

The enemy appeared in strength at 7 a.m. Because of faulty shells, the Parrotts were advanced to be in line with the other batteries, which opened fire at 7:30. Heavy cannonading continued until 10:30. The enemy pressure continued to build and the Confederates were forced to fall back, the artillery withdrawing in good order by sections through the woods. They then went into position in support of Brigadier General X. B. Debray's Texas cavalry brigade and continued to engage the enemy, the ten guns firing a total of 314 rounds. During the engagement, the 1st Regulars had one private and one horse slightly wounded by shell fragments.

On May 18, the Confederates moved forward to Bayou de Glaize as the enemy forces neared the Mississippi River. Taking position near a ruined sugar house on Norwood's Plantation on the extreme left of the line at 2 p.m., the battalion come under artillery attack. Opening fire at 3 p.m., it soon silenced the enemy batteries and caused the Union sharpshooters to

---

[62] *OR*, Series I, Vol. XXXIV, Part 1, pp. 570-571, 580, 583-584, 587-588, 596-597. Taylor, *Destruction and Reconstruction*, pp. 186-229. W. H. Parsons, " 'The World Never Witnessed Such Fights,' " *Civil War Times Illustrated*, XXIV, No. 5 (September 1985), pp. 22-23.

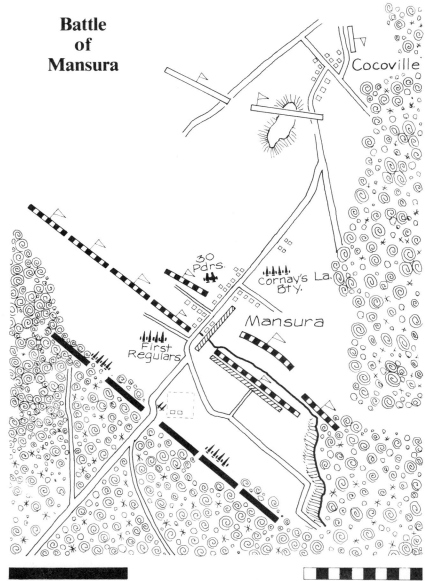

**Battle
of
Mansura**

Cocoville

30 Pdrs.

cornay's La.
Bty.

First
Regulars

Mansura

■■■■■■■■	▨▨▨▨▨▨
2nd Position Confederate	**2nd Position Union**
▨▨▨▨▨▨▨▨	☐
1st Position Confederate	**1st Position Union**

retire. The guns then covered the advance of the Confederate dismounted cavalry, until it was halted by superior enemy numbers. The Confederate guns quickly stopped a Union force and covered the Confederate withdrawal. Barnes' 1st Regulars was the last battery to retire, firing by sections, and silencing the enemy. The action ended about sunset and the Confederate batteries moved to the bayou road. This engagement marked the end of the Red River Campaign. Barnes' battery during the day had fired 17 solid shot and 40 shells from its two bronze James rifles and 8 solid shot and 7 shells from one 12-pounder at ranges varying from 800 to 1,000 yards. The battery did not suffer any casualties.[63]

The close of the Red River Campaign marked the end of significant military operations in the Trans-Mississippi Department. On June 1, 1864, Lieutenant George E. Strawbridge of Company K, 1st Louisiana Heavy Artillery, was assigned to temporary duty with the 1st Regulars. On November 19, the 1st Regulars were assigned to the 3d Field Artillery Battalion (Mounted) which was commanded successively by Majors T. A. Faries and C. W. Squires. It acted as Company A of this battalion until the end of the war. Semmes commanded the 1st Field Artillery Battalion. At the end of the year the 3d Battalion was attached to Major General John H. Forney's First Texas Infantry Division and Semmes' battalion was with the Second Texas Cavalry Division of Brigadier General Samuel B. Maxey. The 1st Regulars, with three 3-inch rifles and three 6-pounders, was at Tyler, Texas, when General E. Kirby Smith surrendered the last Confederate forces on June 2, 1865. Many of the men of the battery, however, were scattered in details throughout the Trans-Mississippi Department. The company was officially paroled at Alexandria on June 4.[64]

Because of the complete lack of muster rolls for the 1st Confederate Light Artillery Battery after August 1862 it is impossible to give an accurate statistical summation of its activities. Mention of the battery in any records during the last year of the war is very scanty. The efficiency and discipline of the battery is often commended by both sides during the war and it seems probable that one reason for this was that three of its officers were West Pointers. From at least 1863, the battery was apparently kept up to strength by the addition of Louisiana volunteers and conscripts. Surviving records show 208 men having served with the battery at one time or another, of whom 137 can be identified as regulars. Two of the regulars had previous United States service. The battery lost according to available records 6 men killed

---

[63] *OR,* Series I, Vol. XXXIV, Part 1, pp. 629-632.

[64] Special Order No. 127, A&IGO, June 1, 1864. *OR,* Series I, Vol. XLI, Part 4, pp. 1064-1065, 1146, and Vol. XLVIII, Part 2, p. 693.

in action or died of wounds, 6 wounded, 29 captured, 2 discharged, 14 deserted, and 2 died in service. There is no record of what finally happened to 71 men, most of them regulars. The battery's distinguished record has remained little known because it served in a backwater of the war.

The Infantry School of Practice battalion was the largest regular Confederate unit raised. From this beginning, its men went on to take part in the defense of the New Orleans river forts, the Battle of Baton Rouge, the campaigns in Louisiana, and the defense of Mobile. The 1st Confederate Light Artillery Battery was one of the best batteries in the Confederate Army while Company C at New Orleans disintegrated after the fall of the city. The men in the 1st Louisiana Heavy Artillery served well until the closing days of the war.

Chapter V

THE MARYLAND CONFEDERATE REGULARS

The first effort at recruiting the Confederate regular army was perhaps the strangest. Louis T. Wigfall, the brilliant and erratic senator from Texas, early in March 1861 proposed to the Confederate War Department that it would be possible to obtain a large number of recruits in Baltimore for the Southern army. On March 5, the day before Congress formally authorized the regular army, Secretary of War Walker approved Wigfall's plan and authorized him to ship recruits to Charleston to be mustered into service.[1] Wigfall promptly opened his cladestine recruiting office behind enemy lines.

William Dorsey Pender had decided to resign his commission as first lieutenant and regimental adjutant of the 1st United States Dragoons. The twenty-seven year old North Carolinian went directly to Montgomery, where he received an appointment as captain in the Corps of Artillery. "I told the Secretary," Pender on March 16 wrote his wife, "that when my company was enlisted I should like to do it myself and he gave me to understand that just now they had no time [to] recruit but in the course of a few weeks they

---

[1] Letter and telegram, Walker to Wigfall, March 5, 1861, Letters Sent, Secretary of War, Chap. IX, Vol. I, pp. 26-28, RG 109, NA.

**GENERAL PIERRE GUSTAVE
TOUTANT BEAUREGARD**
Courtesy of the Casemate Museum

would probably do so."[2] The results of Wigfall's recruiting efforts had proven sufficiently promising and on March 21, General Cooper changed Captain Pender's orders from Pensacola and directed him to proceed secretly to Baltimore and take charge of the recruiting. Concurrently, General Beauregard was notified to expect the arrival of recruits in Charleston.[3]

Pender arrived in Baltimore on March 24 and then went to Washington the following day to see Senator Wigfall. On March 26, he wrote to his wife,

> I am sending men South to be enlisted in the Southern Army. I merely inspect and ship them. I do nothing that the law could take hold of if they wished to trouble me, but Baltimore is strong for secession, and I am backed up by the sympathy of the first men here. ... Do not fear for me whatever you may see in the papers, for rest assured that in the first place I shall be prudent and in the second I am well backed. I do not want my official capacity to be known except by a few who are with us.[4]

The connivance of local officials and the relative success of the recruiting effort are shown in a letter from Pender on April 3. "As to danger, I am not in the least, for not only are the best and larger number of the people with us, but the police is all right. They have been at the boat each time I have sent off men. I sent sixty-one in less than a week. Sixty-four had been sent a few days before I arrived."[5]

Pender was ordered to close his recruiting depot on April 11, the day before the attack on Fort Sumter. In May, he was commissioned colonel of

---

[2] William Hassler (ed.), *The General to His Lady* (Chapel Hill: University of North Carolina Press, 1962), p. 10. Hassler says in two places, pp. viii and 11, that Pender's commission was in the Provisional Army, when in fact it was a regular army commission. See Regular Army Register, Chap. I, Vol. 88, pp. 30-31, RG 109, NA. Hassler also has the peculiar statement that "Pender was sent to Baltimore to take charge of the Confederate security depot."

[3] Cooper to Pender and Cooper to Beauregard, March 21, 1861, Letters Sent, A&IGO, Chap. I, Vol. 35, pp. 10-11, RG 109, NA.

[4] *The General to His Lady*, pp. 11-12.

[5] *Ibid.*, p. 13.

the 13th North Carolina Infantry and had risen to major general by the time he died of wounds following the Battle of Gettysburg. As might be expected, due to the hurried and secret manner of the recruitment effort, some confusion arose. Many recruits arriving in Charleston were found unfit for military service. Also, in Baltimore the men had been promised a bounty for which there was at that time no legal provision.[6] In all, about 125 recruits from Baltimore were accepted for the regular army and were formally enlisted at Castle Pinckney in Charleston Harbor.

Castle Pinckney, located on Shute's Folly Island a mile off the shore of Charleston, was a small casemated brick fort completed in 1809. The Federals had started to repair the old fort in December 1860, but had abandoned it on December 27. Although it mounted some guns, Castle Pinckney was too small and too close to the city to be a major element of the harbor defense, but the Confederates used it first as a training site and later as a prison.[7]

The recruits enlisted by Captain Pender in Baltimore began to arrive in Charleston on March 26. They were assembled at Castle Pinckney under

GARRISON OF SOUTH CAROLINA TROOPS, CASTLE PINCKNEY, CHARLESTON, S.C., AUGUST 1861. *Photo by George S. Cook*
Eleanor S. Brockenbrough Library, The Museum of the Confederacy
Courtesy of the Library of Congress

---

[6] *Ibid*, p. 14. Cooper to Pender, April 1, 1861; Cooper to Beauregard, April 1, 1861; Cooper to Pender, April 8, 1861; Letters Sent, A&IGO, Chap. I, Vol. 35, pp. 10-11, 20-21, 28, RG 109, NA. Cooper to Beauregard, March 22, 1861, Letters and Telegrams to Gen. Beauregard, Chap. II, Vol. 256, p. 62, RG 109, NA. *OR*, Series I, Vol. I, p. 284.

[7] Kenneth E. Lewis and William T. Langhorne, Jr., *Castle Pinckney: An Archaeological Assessment and Recommendations* (Columbia: Institute for Archaeology and Anthropology, University of South Carolina, 1978), pp. 3, 17, 21.

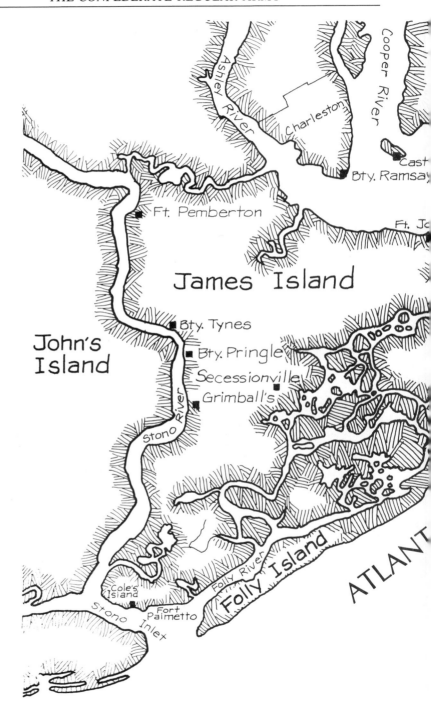

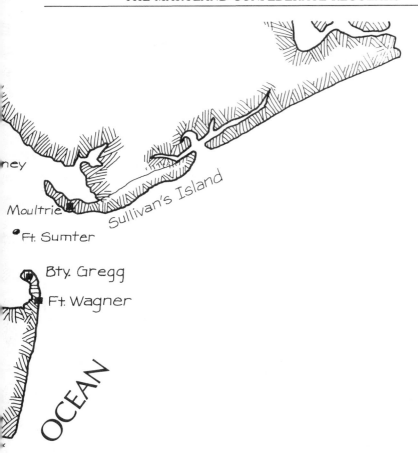

ney

Moultrie

Sullivan's Island

Ft. Sumter

Bty. Gregg

Ft. Wagner

OCEAN

Defenses of
Charleston City
and Harbor

the command of Captain Frederick L. Childs, Corps of Artillery, who had been a second lieutenant in the 1st United States Artillery before resigning on March 4. For some strange reason, the War Department felt that it was not necessary to equip these recruits immediately, although hostilities momentarily could be expected at Fort Sumter just across the harbor from Castle Pinckney. On April 22, Childs was ordered to North Carolina on recruiting duty and First Lieutenant William F. Barnwell, a regular officer from South Carolina, replaced him in command of the recruits.[8]

General Beauregard felt that some use should be made of the regular recruits and on May 1 recommended that they be formed into two artillery companies. The Corps of Artillery was an innovation on the part of the Confederacy. Since 1821 the artillery of the United States Army had been organized into regiments. The companies of these regiments, however, were widely scattered and had never served together under their regimental organization in the field. For many years there had been considerable discussion on the maintenance of this regimental organization and the Confederates decided to abandon it in favor of the corps system. The Confederates also placed all ordnance duties under the Corps of Artillery, another system abandoned by the United States Army. As has been seen, this latter provision did not prove practical and was abandoned in practice if not in theory.

The Corps of Artillery originally was to consist of a colonel, a lieutenant colonel, ten majors, and forty companies of artillerists and artificers Each company was to consist of a captain, 2 first lieutenants, 1 second lieutenant, 4 sergeants, 4 corporals, 2 musicians, and 70 privates. The President was authorized to equip not more than four of the companies as 6-gun light artillery batteries in time of peace. No limitation seems to have been placed on the number of light batteries in war time. In addition, there was a provision for 100 mechanics to be regularly enlisted for ordnance duty.[9]

The Corps of Artillery was to have an adjutant selected from the lieutenants and a sergeant major selected from the enlisted men. By the Act of May 16, 1861, six military storekeepers were added with the rank of first lieutenant.[10] An act of August 21, 1861, authorized the appointment of an additional lieutenant colonel and two majors to the Corps of Artillery and four military storekeepers of ordnance with the rank of captain.[11] An act of April 19, 1862, provided for an increase in ordnance sergeants so that

---

[8] Capt. Stephen D. Lee to Cooper, March 26, 1861, and Beauregard to Cooper, April 1, 1861, Register of Letters Received, A&IGO, Chap. I, Vol. 45, pp. 123, 19, RG 109, NA. Childs to Cooper, April 9, 1861, and Cooper to Beauregard, April 9, 1861, Letters Sent, A&IGO, Chap. I, Vol. 35, p. 29, RG 109, NA.

[9] *Statutes*, Chapter XXIV, Sections 5 and 23.

[10] *Ibid.*, Chapter XX, Section 3, and Chapter XXIV, Section 8.

[11] *Ibid.*, Chapter XXXIV, Section 1.

there would be one for each regiment. Although written so that it applied to the regular army, it seems to have been actually used for the Provisional Army.[12]

Beauregard's request to form two companies of the Corps of Artillery was approved on May 3 and he was given discretion in assigning the officers to the units. As with the rest of the regular army, the Corps of Artillery was never recruited up to strength. In addition to the two companies at Charleston, only one additional regular company — the 1st Confederate Light Artillery Battery described in the previous chapter — was formed in Louisiana the following year.[13] On June 12, Captain Childs recommended that the recruits in North Carolina be sent to the artillery companies in Charleston. Captain Alfred Iverson was ordered to forward the ten North Carolina recruits from Fort Johnston at the mouth of the Cape Fear River.[14]

The two artillery companies were organized on May 11 with Captains Stephen D. Lee and Charles S. Winder in command. Lee, a South Carolinian, had been a first lieutenant in the 4th United States Artillery and had served as Beauregard's quartermaster in Charleston. Winder was from Maryland and had been a captain in the 9th United States Infantry. Although commissioned a captain in the Corps of Artillery, the War Department eventually changed Winder's rank to major, but this apparently did not get straightened until after he left the Charleston company. Originally assigned to Winder's Company were First Lieutenant Benjamin F. Sloan, Jr., a former second lieutenant in the 2d United States Dragoons, and Lieutenant Barnwell. Subsequently Second Lieutenants Joseph G. Blount, who had been a cadet at West Point when the war began, and Theodore B. Hayne of South Carolina were attached to the company. With Lee's Company were First Lieutenant Samuel C. Williams and Second Lieutenant John F. O'Brien, both recently resigned West Point cadets.[15]

The terrain provided many natural advantages for the defense of Charleston as well as presenting some problems. The city was situated on a narrow peninsula between the Ashley and Cooper Rivers, which united to form Charleston Harbor. To the south lies James Island, which is divided

---

[12] *Ibid*, Statute II, Chapter XLIII.

[13] Beauregard to Cooper, May 1, 1861, Register of Letters Received, A&IGO, Chap. I, Vol. 45, p. 26, and Cooper to Beauregard, May 3, 1861, Letters Sent, A&IGO, Chap. I, Vol. 35, p. 91, RG 109, NA.

[14] Childs to Cooper, June 12, 1861, Register of Letters Received, A&IGO, Chap. I, Vol. 45, p. 39; R. H. Chilton to Iverson, July 4, 1861, Letters Sent, A&IGO, Chap. I, Vol. 35, p. 236; Childs, June 12, 1861, ordering Lance Sergeant Isaac Marsh to proceed with recruits from Wilmington to Fort Johnston, *CMSR*, Capt. F. L. Childs, Childs' Company South Carolina Artillery; Special Order No. 34, Fort Johnson [sic], N.C., July 7, 1861, transferring ten recruits to Charleston, *CMSR*, Col. Alfred Iverson, 20th North Carolina Infantry; RG 109, NA. For additional information on recruiting in North Carolina, see Chapter II.

[15] Special Order No. 111, Provisional Army, Charleston, S.C., May 11, 1861; Muster Roll, Detachment of Recruits, May 11, 1861; RG 109, NA.

from Johns Island by Stono Inlet and the Stono River. The Stono River is navigable to near the city. Between Stono Inlet and the mouth of the harbor twelve miles away are Folly and Morris Islands, two sandy sea islands about two miles wide. At the northern tip of Morris Island and forming the southern edge of the harbor is Cummings Point. About 2,700 yards to the north is Sullivan's Island. The original Federal defenses of the harbor consisted of Castle Pinckney on Shute's Folly Island near the city, Fort Moultrie on Sullivan's Island, Fort Sumter on an artificial island midway between Cummings Point and Sullivan's Island, and Fort Johnson on the harbor shore of James Island behind Fort Sumter. The Confederates immediately began the construction of earthwork fortifications along the Stono River to protect the rear approach to the city. The right of this line was Fort Pemberton, near Wappoo Cut, a large heavily armed fortification. The line continued down the Stono with Battery Tynes and Battery Pringle. On Cole's Island, a small sand island in Stono Inlet, was Fort Palmetto. Battery Gaines was erected on Cummings Point to protect the rear of Fort Sumter and the larger Battery Wagner was placed near the south end of Morris Island to prevent an enemy advance along the shore. Most of the area between the sand islands along the sea and the harbor consisted of marsh which made military operations virtually impossible. As the war progressed, additional batteries were built behind the marshes, along the shore of Sullivan's Island, and along the shore of Charleston proper. While the strong forts and marshes made siege operations extremely difficult, the great length of the defensive line strained Confederate resources.

Winder's Company was ordered immediately to Charleston Arsenal, locate on the north side of the city. Lee's Company remained at Castle Pinckney until it was ordered on May 23 to Fort Palmetto on Cole's Island. The company left Castle Pinckney on May 30, leaving one noncommissioned officer and ten men under the command of Lieutenant Blount, and arrived at Cole's Island on June 1. Captain Lee was detailed from the company on various assignments and command again reverted to Lieutenant Barnwell. Lieutenant Williams was transferred to Virginia in September and Lee was promoted to major in the Provisional Army in November and followed him. Lee eventually rose to the rank of lieutenant general and commanded a corps in the Army of Tennessee. Williams became a temporary major in the regular army and commanded an artillery battalion in the Army of Tennessee. Lieutenant Barnwell apparently died November 23, 1861, and Lieutenant Hayne succeeded to the command of the company.[16]

---

[16] General Order No. 39, Provisional Army, Charleston, S.C., May 23, 1861; Muster Roll, Capt. Lee's Company of Artillery, June 30, 1861; Maj. J. Jonathan Lucas, February 17, 1864, enclosure to J. W. Hayne to James A. Seddon, February 23, 1864, *CMSR*, Capt. T. B. Hayne, 15th South Carolina Heavy Artillery Battalion; RG 109, NA.

At the time of their organization, Winder's Company consisted of sixty men and Lee's Company of seventy-eight. In addition to Winder's Company, there were also at Charleston Arsenal at the end of June two unassigned recruits and Master Blacksmith James O'Neill who had enlisted in the Ordnance Department. Winder was not happy in Charleston. On June 27, he wrote the War Department requesting to be promoted in the Provisional Army and transferred or to have his company ordered to active duty. On July 8, he accepted a commission as colonel of the 6th South Carolina Infantry. Winder was eventually promoted to brigadier general, commanding the Stonewall Brigade in the Army of Northern Virginia. He was killed in action at Cedar Mountain in 1862. Captain Childs was assigned to command the Charleston Arsenal and on July 26, 1861, he was notified that he had also succeeded Winder in command of the artillery company.[17]

On October 25, fifty men of Childs' Company, under the command of Lieutenant O'Brien, left Charleston Arsenal for detached duty at Fort Sumter. Differences in inspection reports of the two companies during this period are interesting. The military appearance of Lee's Company was reported as "magnificent" while Childs' Company only rated a "tolerable." Lee's Company was rated as good as far as discipline and instruction while the best that could be said about Childs' Company was that they were improving. The reasons for these differences may be that Captain Childs had to devote most of his time to ordnance duties while Lieutenant Hayne and his men were actually in the field.[18]

From Fort Sumter, O'Brien's detachment was ordered on January 25, 1862, to join Captain William C. Preston's Company A, 1st South Carolina Artillery, which was serving as field artillery, at Simons Farm on James Island. The company struck camp at Simons Farm on February 25 and marched nine miles to Camp Verdier. Lee's Company was withdrawn from Cole's Island on May 12 when Major General John C. Pemberton, the new department commander, ordered the abandonment of the fortifications at the mouth of the Stono. The company probably moved to Fort Pemberton up the Stono River on James Island. Childs' Company was reunited and in August was transferred from Charleston Arsenal to Fort Pemberton. On November 15, the War Department decided that both companies were so reduced in size that they should be consolidated. The companies had pro-

[17] Post Return, Charleston Arsenal, June 1861; Winder to Cooper, June 27, 1861, and Maj. J. Gorgas to Cooper, July 11, 1861, Register of Letters Received, A&IGO, Chap. I, Vol. 34, pp. 260, 202; R. H. Chilton to Childs, July 26, 1861, Letters Sent, A&IGO, Chap. I, Vol. 35, p. 285; RG 109, NA. Warner, *Generals in Gray*, pp. 339-340.

[18] Post Return, Charleston Arsenal, October 1861; Muster Roll, Capt. Stephen D. Lee's Company of Artillery, December 31, 1861; Muster Roll, Capt. Frederick L. Childs' Company, Corps of Artillery, August 31, 1861; RG 109, NA.

**LIEUTENANT GENERAL
JOHN C. PEMBERTON**
Courtesy of the Casemate Museum

bably been under the operational command of Hayne since August. The consolidated company was then attached to the 15th South Carolina Heavy Artillery Battalion, commanded by Major J. Jonathan Lucas.[19]

Lucas' battalion had originally consisted of two companies of state regulars.[20] After the Confederate regular company joined Lucas' battalion, it was kept up to strength with South Carolina conscripts. Hayne had requested on March 30 that, since it was obvious that Captain Lee would never return to the company, that he be promoted to captain in the Provisional Army. Hayne finally received a promotion to temporary captain in the regular army on November 7 and officially took command of the consolidated unit, redesignated a week later as Company C, 15th South Carolina Heavy Artillery Battalion. The day before, Stephen D. Lee had been promoted to brigadier general at Vicksburg. Childs had been promoted to temporary major on August 1, and subsequently commanded the Charleston, Augusta, and Fayetteville Arsenals, becoming lieutenant colonel of the 2d North Carolina Local Defense Troops in 1863.[21]

The new Company C consisted of 4 officers, 6 sergeants, 7 corporals, and 88 privates. In addition to Hayne, the officers were First Lieutenant John A. Keith and Second Lieutenants Lee M. Butler and W. W. Revely. All held regular commissions. Butler was on detached service with Brigadier General S. R. Gist and probably saw very little service with the company. Of the

---

[19] Muster Roll, Detachment of Capt. F. L. Childs' Company, Corps of Artillery, February 28, 1862; Muster Roll, Capt. Frederick L. Childs' Company, Corps of Artillery, August 27, 1862; Special Order No. 268, A&IGO, November 15, 1862; RG 109, NA. There are no muster rolls for Lee's Company on file after April 30, 1862.

[20] See Chapter I for the difference between Confederate and state regulars.

[21] Hayne to G. W. Randolph, March 30, 1862, *CMSR,* Capt. T. B. Hayne, 15th South Carolina Heavy Artillery Battalion; *CMSR,* Capt. F. L. Childs, Childs' Company, South Carolina Artillery; RG 109, NA. A good example of the forgetfullness of the War Department is the transposition of the abbreviation C.S. Artillery to S.C. Artillery in the consolidation order and all records of the two companies have since been filed as South Carolina organizations. A biographical sketch of Hayne, the son of Attorney General J. W. Hayne of South Carolina, appears in David D. Wallace, *The History of South Carolina* (New York: American Historical Society, Inc., 1934), Vol. IV, p. 887.

previous officers who served with the regulars, Sloan had been promoted and finished the war as an artillery major in North Carolina, Gibson was transferred to Texas and became a captain by the end of the war, Blount had transferred to Virginia and became major of an artillery battalion. O'Brien went to Virginia on Winder's staff and finished the war as a major in the Trans-Mississippi Department. During May and June 1862, First Lieutenant Arthur S. Cunningham of the Corps of Artillery, who had been a staff major, served briefly with the company. Cunningham was promoted to temporary lieutenant colonel in June and went to Virginia. There seems to have always been a shortage of adequate clothing for the company. The small arms carried by the men were a mixed lot, some being ancient smoothbore muskets altered to percussion with a few new Model 1851 Springfield muskets.[22]

The first military threat to the safety of Charleston had materialized when a Union expedition captured Port Royal Sound, midway between the South Carolina port and Savannah, on November 7, 1861. In the following months, the Federals had consolidated their grip on the Port Royal Sound area, threatened the vital Charleston and Savannah Railroad, attempted to blockade Charleston Harbor with the "Stone Fleet," and pushed the occupation of the coast islands nearer the city. The abandonment of Cole's Island had permitted Union warships to enter the Stono River and on June 2 the Federals landed troops on the southern end of James Island. A sharp defeat at the Battle of Secesionville on June 16 resulted in the Union evacuation of James Island in early July. For the remainder of the year, the Federals devoted their attention toward the southern part of South Carolina while the Confederates busily strengthened the defenses of Charleston. General Beauregard had succeeded Pemberton as commander of the Department of South Carolina, Georgia, and Florida in September, and on December 28 a reorganization placed the defenses of the harbor and approaches to Charleston in the First Military District of South Carolina. The district extended from the South Santee River east of the city to the Stono River and Rantowles Creek on the West.[23]

About January 20, 1863, General Beauregard ordered Brigadier General Roswell S. Ripley, the commander of the First Military District, to surprise the enemy's gunboats operating on the Stono River. Ripley proposed to put

[22] Muster Rolls, Company C, 15th South Carolina Heavy Artillery Battalion, December 31, 1862, February 28, 1863, and April 30, 1863, RG 109, NA.

[23] E. Milby Burton, *The Siege of Charleston, 1861-1865* (Columbia: University of South Carolina Press, 1970), pp. 66-119. General Order No. 132, Department of South Carolina, Georgia, and Florida, December 28, 1862, *OR*, Series I, Vol. XIV, p. 736.

eight to ten guns suddenly in position on the west side of the river during the night to cut off the gunboats when they came up stream. Lieutenant Colonel Joseph A. Yates of the 1st South Carolina Artillery was put in command of the project. Yates assembled a large number of rifled siege guns — perhaps as many as thirty — and secretly moved them into position on both sides of the river on the night of January 28, with most of the guns being located on James Island. Part of this force consisted of a detachment of three noncommissioned officers and twelve privates from Company C under Captain Hayne which manned three rifled 24-pounder guns stationed at Thomas Grimball's Plantation on James Island, just down stream from Battery Pringle and on the first solid ground reached coming up the Stono.

CONFEDERATE ARTILLERY NEAR CHARLESTON
Museum of the Confederacy
Courtesy of The Valentine Museum, Richmond, Virginia

For a time after the Confederate guns were in position there was no activity on the river. Finally, at 3 p.m. on January 30, the gunboat U.S.S. *Isaac Smith*, commanded by Acting Lieutenant F. S. Conover, got underway from its anchorage in Stono Inlet and started up river. This screw steamer, purchased by the Navy in 1861 and converted into a gunboat, had taken part in the capture of Port Royal Sound. A little after 4 p.m., Conover anchored opposite Grimball Plantation. His lookout did not spot anything unusual. Captain John H. Gary, commanding the detachment of the 15th South Carolina at Grimball's, waited for about twenty minutes and then, after the enemy showed no disposition to land, opened fire with his three 24-pounders.

His guns were masked behind a thick clump of trees about 600 yards from the Union gunboat. Conover immediately got underway and cleared for action. The gunboat returned the fire from shore with grape, canister, shell, and Parrott shot from her nine guns. A grapeshot struck the gun manned by the regulars under Captain Hayne, but did no damage. The guns hidden on the opposite bank of the Stono on Johns Island also joined in the duel and Conover realized that he was trapped. Conover attempted to run by the hidden batteries, but a shot in the steam chimney stopped the engine, and with no wind, little tide, and boats riddled with shot, the *Isaac Smith* was helpless. Because of the large number of wounded on the berth deck, Conover gave up the idea of blowing up his ship and surrendered. The *Isaac Smith* had eight men killed, one officer mortally wounded, and sixteen sailors wounded during the engagement. One Confederate private of the 18th South Carolina Heavy Artillery Battalion was mortally wounded. The entire crew of the gunboat, consisting of eleven officers and 108 men, was captured and the ship was eventually towed up the Stono and put under the guns of Fort Pemberton. The gunboat U.S.S. *Commodore McDonough* attempted to come up river to aid the *Isaac Smith*, but her captain wisely realized that his ship would probably meet the same fate and, after exchanging a few shots with the batteries, dropped back down stream. The *Isaac Smith* was taken to Charleston, repaired, and entered Confederate service as the *Stono*.[24]

Company C apparently remained at Fort Pemberton during the first half of 1863. The Confederates began fortifying the south end of Morris Island on March 7, soon followed on March 28 by the occupation of Cole's Island and Folly Island by the Federals. On April 7, the Federal ironclads under Rear Admiral Samuel F. DuPont attempted to force the entrance of Charleston Harbor, but a furious battle lasting two and a half hours resulted in five of the eight warships being disabled, one sinking the next morning. During the following two months, both armies conducted raids and scouting expeditions. The Gist Guards, Mathewes Artillery, and Company B, German Artillery, were attached to the 15th South Carolina Heavy Artillery Battalion, but the latter unit was stationed in the Fourth Military District, beyond the South Santee River.

Cumming's Point on Morris Island was the site of Battery Gregg, a substantial sand battery located 1,390 yards from Fort Sumter. It was designed as an outwork of Fort Sumter, to protect its rear from fire coming from the main ship channel, as well as from the land side of Morris and James Islands. Morris Island, a strip of low lying sand hillocks, stretched from Cumming's

[24] *OR*, Series I, Vol. XIV, pp. 203-204. *ORN*, Series I, Vol. 13, pp. 558-559, 563-566. Muster Roll, Company C, 15th South Carolina Heavy Artillery Battalion, February 28, 1863, RG 109, NA. *Dictionary of American Fighting Ships*, Vol. III, pp. 462-463. Burton, *Siege of Charleston*, pp. 120-123.

Point flat, narrow, and open to view for one half of its length of nearly four miles. The southern half of the island widens and rises in sand hills of from thirty to forty feet above sea level. Within the range of Fort Sumter's guns, 2,780 yards distant, and located immediately to command the narrowest part of the island, stood Battery Wagner. This fortification extended completely across the island, with a front of 250 yards. On July 10, 1863, Union forces stormed the southern half of Morris Island and the following day were repulsed in an attempt to carry Battery Wagner. After a tremendous bombardment, another assault was made on Battery Wagner on July 18, but this was repulsed with heavy casualties. Company C was transferred to Battery Wagner and replaced part of its weary garrison from July 27 to July 31 and then was shifted to Fort Johnson, on the harbor side of James Island, finally returning to Fort Pemberton on August 1.[25]

The enemy began a massive bombardment of Fort Sumter with large rifled guns on August 17. At the same time, a steady fire was maintained against Battery Wagner by both the siege batteries and the ironclad gunboats of the fleet. The exposed position and constant strain on the garrison of Battery Wagner under these conditions required frequent rotations of the units manning the defenses. Company C left Fort Pemberton on August 20 and early the following morning returned to Battery Wagner as part of the relief garrison commanded by Brigadier General Johnson Hagood. On August 22, the fleet subjected Battery Wagner to enfilade fire to which it was not able to reply. Early the next morning Hagood opened fire on siege lines which were drawing closer to Battery Wagner. During the day the land batteries and the U.S.S. *New Ironsides* bombarded the battery, the return fire doing slight damage to the enemy ship. That evening Lieutenant Keith of Company C was evacuated because of sickness, leaving important guns in the work in charge of noncommissioned officers.

August 24 was to be a grim day for the regulars of Company C. Battery Wagner kept up a steady fire on the advanced siege lines with an 8-inch siege howitzer mounted in the salient. During the morning, the enemy returned this fire with three 300-pounder Parrott guns about 800 yards distant and a battery of 200-pounder Parrotts. The counterbattery fire was so intense that men of Captain W. H. Kennedy's company of the 2d South Carolina Artillery could not be induced to man the howitzer. Under heavy fire, Second Lieutenant Francis C. Lucas, a Provisional Army officer who had been assigned to the company on April 1, and a detachment of regulars from

25 John Johnson, *The Defense of Charleston Harbor* (Charleston: Walker, Evans & Cogswell Co., 1890), pp. 44-61, 81-82, 88-96. Muster Rolls, Company C, 15th South Carolina Heavy Artillery Battalion, June 30, 1863, and August 31, 1863, RG 109, NA. *OR*, Series I, Vol. XXVIII, Part 1, p. 375, and Part 2, pp. 161-162, 248-249. Burton, *Siege of Charleston*, pp. 135-150.

**APPEARANCE PRESENTED BY THE DITCH AND THE SOUTHERN
SLOPE OF BATTERY WAGNER, THE MORNING AFTER THE ASSAULT,
JULY 11, 1863.** *Drawing by Frank Vizetelly.*
Museum of the Confederacy
Courtesy of The Houghton Library, Harvard College Library,
Harvard University, Cambridge, Massachusetts

Company C manned the damaged howitzer and fought it until the gun was
dismounted and ruined by a 200-pounder bolt striking it full in the face. During the fighting on this day, five privates of the company were wounded,
two of them mortally.

Heavy fire continued against Battery Wagner for the next two days and
attacks were launched against the outlying rifle pits. Company C, with a total
strength of seventy-six, was withdrawn on the night on August 26 when the
garrison of the battery was again rotated. It may have fallen back to Battery
Gregg, as seven men are shown to have been wounded there on that day.
Two other privates had been mortally wounded during the period when the
company was at Battery Wagner. By the end of the month, Company C was
back at Fort Pemberton, having suffered 2 officers wounded, 4 privates mortally wounded, and 15 privates wounded. The Union siege lines continued
to advance, and on the night of September 6 the Confederates were finally
forced to abandon Morris Island in order to save the troops manning the
defenses. Company C may have returned to the island just prior to its evacuation, as two privates were captured when the Confederates withdrew.

With Morris Island finally captured, the Union fleet attempted an amphibious attack on Fort Sumter during the night of September 9 with disastrous results.[26]

On October 21, Major Lucas forwarded a recommendation by Captain Hayne that another enemy gunboat operating on the Stono near Grimball's might be ambushed in the same fashion as the *Isaac Smith* had been in January. After considerable discussion it was decided that the circumstances were not as favorable as in the former case, but an attempt might be made. Apparently the enemy did not give the Confederates another opportunity to attempt an ambush. While the debate on the feasibility of this operation continued, the second major bombardment of Fort Sumter began, which lasted from October 26 to December 5.[27]

In December, the company was stationed at Battery Pringle on James Island. Battery Pringle occupied the right of the new and powerful lines built in advance of Fort Pemberton. The battery had been built to dispute the Stono against enemy armored vessels. Captain John J. Allen, who inspected the artillery on James Island at this time, reported that Company C in military appearance, drill, and discipline was first class. The company's muskets, garrison equipage, and accoutrements were in good order and police of the camp was good. The company at this time had 2 officers, 6 noncommissioned officers, and 64 privates present for duty. Their rations consisted of beef and corn meal. In the three months following the December inspection there was a radical change in the company. On January 14, 1864, Privates Michael Boyle and Cornelius Hearlehay, while on guard at Battery Pringle, stole the picket boat in the Stono River and deserted.[28] The company moved on March 28 to Battery Ramsay, located at the tip of the city of Charleston. At the end of April discipline was reported not to be good. Two sergeants and four privates had deserted during the month and one corporal and seventeen of the regular privates were confined in the Charleston jail.[29]

The reason for this sudden collapse of discipline in what, by all inspection reports and comments of senior officers, was an excellent unit may be traced to an inconsistant War Department policy. As late as February 17,

---

[26] *OR*, Series I, Vol. XXVIII, Part 1, pp. 384-396, 437-444, 499. Johnson, *Defense of Charleston*, pp. 147-151, Appendix A, pp. x-xi. Burton, *Siege of Charleston*, pp. 151-180. Muster Roll, Company C, 15th South Carolina Heavy Artillery Battalion, August 31, 1863, RG 109, NA.

[27] *OR*, Series I, Vol. XXVIII, Part 2, pp. 435-438.

[28] Both had been wounded in the fighting at Battery Wagner.

[29] Warren Ripley (ed.), *Siege Train, the Journal of a Confederate Artilleryman in the Defense of Charleston* (Columbia: University of South Carolina Press, 1986), pp. 110, 115, 117-119. *OR*, Series I, Vol. XXVIII, Part 2, p. 599, and Vol. XXXV, Part 1, p. 134. Johnson, *Defense of Charleston*, pp. 215, 221. Muster Rolls, Company C, 15th South Carolina Heavy Artillery Battalion, February 29, 1864, and April 30, 1864, RG 109, NA.

Major Lucas in recommending Hayne for promotion described the company as the most efficient in the service. Lucas expected the company to disband in March when the three year enlistments of the regulars expired. But the War Department in the case of Company C maintained that the men could be held in service under the conscription act. In the case of the regular cavalry company which had been recruited in Texas at the same time, this position was not taken and the men who refused to reenlist had been discharged. When the men of Company C learned the War Department decision, they were on the verge of mutiny and the company had to be withdrawn from the front lines to Charleston. It appears that many of the regulars did want to continue to serve, but most of them were Marylanders and desired to leave Charleston and join units operating nearer to home.[30]

This unpleasant situation was in part remedied. A plan had been approved by the War Department, mainly at the instigation of Colonel Bradley T. Johnson, to organize a unit known as the Maryland Line. Johnson, a prominent Maryland politician before the war, had served with distinction as colonel of the 1st Maryland Infantry. In addition to Maryland units already serving in the Army of Northern Virginia, all citizens of Maryland serving in units from other states would be transferred at their request to the Maryland Line. The Maryland Line had originally been authorized on February 26, 1862, but apparently no great effort had been made to organize the force. The War Department directed Major General Arnold Elzey, a West Pointer from Maryland, to take command of the Maryland Line and to organize Camp Maryland at Staunton, Virginia. Elzey, a lieutenant colonel in the Confederate regular army, had been severely wounded during the Seven Days Campaign and had since been limited to duty as commander of the Department of Richmond. At the same time, Colonel Johnson assumed command of Camp Howard near Hanover Junction, Virginia, where the remainder of the Maryland Line was to gather.

George P. Kane, the former marshal of the Baltimore police department, served as a volunteer aide to General Elzey in attempting to organize the Maryland Line. Word had reached him of the unrest among the Marylanders at Charleston and he quickly journeyed south. Kane conferred with Generals Beauregard and Ripley and they acknowledged the justice of the transfer order. Both generals bore testimony to the bravery and devotion of these men to the Confederate cause. According to Kane, some 500 or 600 men from Maryland had come to Charleston before the attack on Fort Sumter,

---

[30] *CMSR*, Capt. T. B. Hayne, 15th South Carolina Heavy Artillery Battalion, RG 109, NA. Lucas' comments regarding the company were seconded by Col. C. H. Simonton, commanding James Island, and Brig. Gen. William B. Taliaferro, commanding the district. A good presentation of the attitude of the men and the official position taken in regard to holding the men in service appears in a letter of Sgt. Frederick F. Crate with endorsements, March 29, 1864, *CMSR*, Sgt. Frederick F. Crate, 15th South Carolina Heavy Artillery Battalion, RG 109, NA. Apparently only two of the regulars reenlisted during this period.

so it appears the regular army recruiting effort in Baltimore was small compared to that of South Carolina. It is certain that there were many Marylanders assigned to South Carolina volunteer units around Charleston, but the number remaining in 1864 is not known. Kane maintained that a board of officers convened to consider the complains of the Marylanders decided that the men were entitled to discharge, having served out their full term of enlistment. From information contained in the records of the regulars of Company C this does not seem to be true. Kane and one of Beauregard's staff visited the men under arrest for demanding their discharges, and at Kane's urging they resumed their duty with the promise that they would be transferred to the Maryland Line. On April 29, an order was issued transferring forty-two men of Company C along with many men from other units to the Maryland Line.[31]

On May 15, Lieutenant Revely of Company C was ordered to proceed to Virginia in charge of the men transferred to the Maryland Line from Company C, 15th South Carolina Heavy Artillery Battalion; Company B, 1st South Carolina Artillery; and the Gist Guards. Twenty-six of the men of Company C are known to have arrived in Richmond and to have drawn a clothing issue on May 21. Of the others transferred to the Maryland Line, four remained with Company C and seven apparently were not regulars and their transfer may have been subsequently revoked. After leaving Richmond, the men were taken to Camp Maryland at Staunton, where General Elzey was trying to organize the Maryland Line. Fourteen of the men were assigned to the 2d Maryland Cavalry Battalion, commanded by the famous guerrilla leader Major Harry Gilmore. Others were assigned to the 1st Maryland Cavalry and the 2d and the 4th (Chesapeake) Maryland Artillery Batteries. Gilmore's battalion was operating farther down the Shenandoah Valley, and it seems unlikely that the men actually joined that unit before being rushed into combat.

Major General David Hunter had begun to advance up the Shenandoah Valley on May 26 with an overwhelming Union force. All available men were hastily gathered under the command of Brigadier Generals William E. Jones, John D. Imboden, and John C. Vaughan. Included in this force were 30 Maryland artillerymen from Charleston and about fifty men of Gilmore's battalion. It can not be determined which group the regulars served with, but it seems logical that with their previous experience they should have been in the artillery detachment. They were thrown into a hopeless engagement at Piedmont, seven miles southwest of Port Republic, on June 5 where Jones' forces were decimated. General Jones was killed and among the 1,500 Con-

31 *OR*, Series IV, Vol. I, pp. 953-954, and Vol. III, pp. 248, 311-312, 510-512. Special Order No. 100, A&IGO, April 29, 1864, RG 109, NA. Warner, *Generals in Gray*, pp. 82-83, 156-157.

federate casualties, seven of the regulars assigned to the 2d Maryland Cavalry Battalion were captured and one was wounded. General Elzey in disgust wrote the War Department that the entire plan to form the Maryland Line was a failure and should be revoked.[32]

The subsequent fate of the men transferred to Virginia was just as bad as their first taste of combat at Piedmont. Two more men were captured during Lieutenant General Jubal Early's subsequent campaign in Maryland. Three men assigned to Gilmore's battalion were captured on August 7 when a Union force surprised Brigadier General Bradley T. Johnson's camp near Moorefield, West Virginia. By the end of the war, all of the men transferred from Company C had been captured or deserted. Five of the men subsequently joined United States Volunteer infantry regiments formed from prisoners of war to fight the Indians.[33]

Meanwhile, back in Charleston, all the problems regarding the Marylanders had apparently not been solved. On June 15, Major General Sam Jones, who had succeeded Beauregard in command of the department, reported to General Cooper that many men of the 1st South Carolina Artillery and Lucas' battalion firmly believed that they were held in service illegally and were greatly dissatisfied, desertions to the enemy being frequent. President Davis advised Jones to inquire into the claims of the men and if they were plausible, to treat them with respectful attention. George P. Kane wrote to the War Department on June 24 complaining about the treatment of the Marylanders still in Charleston and that General Elzey was not receiving the necessary cooperation to organize the Maryland Line. In replying to another complaint a month later, Secretary of War James A. Seddon expressed little sympathy with the position of the Marylanders and that appears to have ended the matter. Despite the unrest in Lucas' battalion, apparently only two regulars from Company C deserted during this period.[34]

After the departure of the men transferred to the Maryland Line, thirteen regular army enlisted men remained with Company C, 15th South Carolina Heavy Artillery Battalion. The remainder of the company, which totalled about fifty men, was not principally composed of South Carolina volunteers and conscripts. The company continued to man the 11-inch and 10-inch guns in Battery Ramsay in Charleston until July 2. The Union commanders had not been idle during this time. A plan had been developed for

---

[32] Special Order No. 134, Department of South Carolina, Georgia, and Florida, May 14, 1864; Clothing Receipt Roll No. 2574; RG 109, NA. Marshall Moore Price, *Conquest of a Valley* (Charlottesville: The University Press of Virginia, 1965), pp. 29, 35, 57-58. OR, Series I, Vol. XL, Part 2, p. 650.

[33] OR, Series I, Vol. XLIII, Part 1, pp. 2-8. See Brown, *Galvanized Yankees,* for the organization and service of the United States Volunteers.

[34] OR, Series I, Vol. XXXV, Part 1, pp. 120-121, and Vol. LIII, p. 341; and Series IV, Vol. III, pp. 510-512, 550-551.

a concerted movement to capture Fort Johnson and Battery Simkins on the James Island shore of Charleston Harbor. While this attack was taking place, demonstrations were to be made on James Island, Johns Island, and the railroad between Charleston and Savannah. The Navy, with two monitors and some gunboats, was assigned the duty of engaging Battery Pringle.

Enemy troops advanced on the southern tip of James Island on the morning of July 2. A large gunboat was driven off by Battery Pringle and the land attack was not pressed vigorously. General Taliaferro, commanding the Seventh Military District which since October 1863 embraced James Island, was sufficiently alarmed to request the return of Captain Hayne and his company to Battery Pringle that night. Company C was promptly ordered back to its former post.[35]

Early the following morning, the enemy attempted an amphibious assault on Fort Johnson which was repulsed with heavy losses. Taliaferro then realized that the activity on the Stono was a diversion to draw troops away from Fort Johnson. Nevertheless, he had a real fight on his hands along the river. The monitors *Lehigh* and *Montauk*, the sloop of war *Pawnee*, the *Commodore McDonough*, and the mortar schooner *Racer*, with troop transports attempted to move up the Stono. Battery Pringle came under severe fire during the morning of July 3. In the fighting this day two of the regular privates of Company C were killed in action. Independence Day was celebrated by the Union forces with a day long bombardment of Battery Pringle. The little fortification continued to receive heavy fire on the following days. General Taliaferro reported on July 8, "The enemy, with two monitors and his fleet of wooden gunboats, opened a terrific fire on Battery Pringle, which was continued for several hours without intermission, causing no serious damage to the work, but with extraordinary accuracy of fire disabling several guns. The fire was returned with spirit by the garrison." That night Company C and the rest of the garrison were withdrawn after a week under almost incessant bombardment and replaced by fresh troops. General Taliaferro in his report of the operations commended Captain Hayne and Lieutenants Revely and Thomas E. Lucas, who had joined the company in December 1863, for gallantry under fire. Company C was soon transferred back to its old station at Fort Pemberton.[36]

The third and final bombardment of Fort Sumter began on July 7 and lasted until September 4. Company C remained at Fort Pemberton until it

[35] Johnson, *Defense of Charleston*, pp. 214-216. *OR*, Series I, Vol. XXXV, Part 1, p. 158, and Part 2, p. 548. Burton, *Siege of Charleston*, pp. 285-286. Ripley, *Siege Train*, pp. 191-196.

[36] Johnson, *Defense of Charleston*, pp. 216-221. *OR*, Series I, Vol. XXXV, Part 1, pp. 166-170. Muster Roll, Company C, 15th South Carolina Heavy Artillery Battalion, August 31, 1864; *CMSR*, William Brass and Gabriel Marty, 15th South Carolina Heavy Artillery Battalion; RG 109, NA. *NOR*, Series I, Vol. 15, p. 555. Burton, *Siege of Charleston*, pp. 286-292. Ripley, *Siege Train*, pp. 196-200.

shifted on October 16 to Battery Tynes, just upstream from Battery Pringle. Minor harrassment by the Union forces continued during the following months, but there were no more serious attempts to take the city by force. On December 28, the 15th South Carolina Heavy Artillery Battalion became part of Colonel Edward C. Anderson's Brigade, Taliaferro's Division. With the advance of Sherman's army through central South Carolina, the Confederate authorities decided to withdraw the troops from Charleston before they were cut off.[37]

The garrison of Charleston, under the command of Lieutenant General William J. Hardee, evacuated the city on February 17, 1865, and fell back to Cheraw, South Carolina. Hardee pressed on into North Carolina to join forces with General Joseph E. Johnston and the Army of Tennessee. The 15th South Carolina Heavy Artillery Battalion had been placed in Colonel Alfred Rhett's brigade of Taliaferro's Division during the retreat. Also in the brigade were the 1st South Carolina Artillery and the 1st South Carolina Infantry, both units of state regulars. In a bitter delaying action near Averasborough, North Carolina, on March 16, Hardee's troops attacked the Fourteenth and Twentieth Corps of Sherman's army. Three regulars of Company C were captured in this fight. By the time the Army of Tennessee surrendered on April 26, only seven regulars of Company C were left in the Confederate service. Fourteen of the regulars, including those transferred from the company, were held as prisoners of war at the end of hostilities. Five others had enlisted in the United States Volunteers after their capture.[38]

On the whole the service of this company of the Confederate regular army was creditable. Repeatedly senior officers commented on the efficiency and courage of the company. During its service, Company C lost in addition to the prisoners of war previously mentioned, 2 men killed in action, 4 men dead of wounds, 2 men died while prisoners of war, and 4 men died of other causes. In addition, two officers and fifteen men were wounded. A total of fifty men deserted, half of these in 1861. There is no final record of what happened to fifteen men. Two were honorably discharged and three dishonorably discharged. There is no record of where 37 of the men were born, but 34 were natives of Maryland and 23 were foreign born, the largest number being from Ireland. Only Sergeant Morris Newman, a native of Missouri, had previous United States regular army service. Except for the unfortunate situation which arose when the men were held in service at the end of their enlistments, the record of the Maryland regulars was probably as good as that of any unit in the Confederate Army.

---

[37] Muster Roll, Company C, 15th South Carolina Heavy Artillery Battalion, October 31, 1864, RG 109, NA. *OR*, Series I, Vol. XLIV, p. 997.

[38] *OR*, Series I, Vol. XLVII, Part 1, pp. 1084-1086, and Part 3, p. 732. Parole Roll No. 526, Greensboro, N.C., RG 109, NA.

Chapter VI

THE CONFEDERATE REGULAR ENGINEERS

When the Confederacy set about to create a regular Army in March 1861 provision was made for a Corps of Engineers. Congress created the regular army in an act passed on March 6, 1861. The Corps of Engineers was to consist of a colonel, four majors, five captains, and a company of sappers, miners, and pontoniers.[1] The company was supposed to be capable of serving in detachments to oversee and aid laborers on fortifications and other Engineer works and to act as fort keepers of finished fortifications to prevent injury and make repairs. The company was to be commanded by one of the captains, assisted by lieutenants detailed from the line. On May 16, Congress passed another act expanding the Corps of Engineers by the addition of a lieutenant colonel and five captains. The following day, Congress authorized a company of sappers and bombardiers for the Corps of Engineers. There is no indication why the two Engineer companies were titled differently. The second company was to consist of a captain, 2 first lieutenants, 1 second lieutenant, 10 sergeants, 10 corporals, 2 musicians, 39 first class privates, and 39 second class privates. The company was to be instructed to perform the same duties as the company authoriz-

---

[1] *Statutes*, Chapter XXIX, Section 1. See Chapter I for details of the act.

ed on March 6. This act in effect added a captain and three lieutenants to the authorized strength of the Corps of Engineers.[2]

Major Josiah Gorgas, Corps of Artillery and Chief of Ordnance, became Acting Chief of Engineers on April 8, 1861. Gorgas was not happy with this additional duty as he had problems enough trying to meet the ordnance requirements of the Confederacy. Finally, on August 3, he was replaced by Major Danville Leadbetter, Corps of Engineers, who had been busy up to that time working on the defenses of Mobile. Strangely both of the first two Chiefs of Engineers were Northerners — Gorgas from Pennsylvania and Leadbetter from Maine. On November 13, Leadbetter returned to Mobile and Captain Alfred L. Rives, Provisional Army, took over direction of the Engineer Bureau.

Jeremy F. Gilmer was promoted from major to lieutenant colonel on September 30, 1862, and on September 25 arrived in Richmond to take over the duty of Chief of Engineers. Gilmer was promoted to the colonelcy of the Corps of Engineers on October 4, one of the few instances of promotions in the regular army during the war. He was another West Pointer and had been General Albert Sidney Johnston's chief engineer at Shiloh. In 1863 he was promoted to major general in the Provisional Army and served as chief engineer of the Department of Northern Virginia and in laying out the defenses in Charleston and Atlanta. During his many absences from the Bureau of Engineers, Rives, who had been promoted to colonel in the Provisional Army, often served as Acting Chief.[3]

Most of the other regular Engineer officers attained the rank of general in the Provisional Army. Major William H. C. Whiting became a major general, commanded a division in the Army of Northern Virginia, and was mainly responsible for the design of Fort Fisher, North Carolina, where he was mortally wounded on January 15, 1865. Major Martin L. Smith was a major general and helped design the defenses of Vicksburg and commanded a division there. He later served as chief engineer of the Military Division of the West. Major Walter H. Stevens became a brigadier general and chief engineer of the Army of Northern Virginia. Major Leadbetter became a brigadier general and was in charge of the engineer work at Mobile after service with the Army of Tennessee. Captain William R. Boggs was a brigadier general and chief of staff to General E. Kirby Smith in the Trans-Mississippi Department. Captain E. Porter Alexander became a brigadier general and Chief of Artillery in Longstreet's Corps, Army of Northern Virginia. Cap-

---

2 Nichols, *Confederate Engineers*, pp. 9-10. *Statutes*, Chapter XX, Section 3, and Chapter XXVIII.

3 Warner, *Generals in Gray*, p. 105. Nichols, *Confederate Engineers*, pp. 10-11, 23-25. OR, Series IV, Vol. I, p. 531.

tain G. W. Custis Lee, the son General Robert E. Lee, rose to major general and commanded a division in his father's army.[4]

Of the remaining regular Engineer officers, Captain Samuel H. Lockett became a colonel and chief engineer of the Department of Alabama, Mississippi, and East Louisiana. Captain Charles R. Collins served as colonel of the 15th Virginia Cavalry and was killed in action at Todd's Tavern on May 7, 1864. Captain Joseph C. Ives was a colonel and aide-de-camp to President Jefferson Davis. Captain William H. Echols became a major and chief engineer of the Department of South Carolina, Georgia, and Florida.

It has been suggested that the regular Engineer company authorized on March 6, 1861, was formed at Knoxville by Captain George R. Margraves and Edmund Winston, but an examination of the records of this company in the National Archives shows no basis for this assumption.[5] Apparently the regular company originally authorized was never formed.

It may be assumed with some certainty that a unit known as Gallimard's Company of Sappers and Bombardiers became the regular company authorized under the Act of May 17, 1861. The exact classification of Gallimard's Company has been a matter of dispute, apparently since the Civil War. Louisiana claimed it as a state unit and there are Confederate orders referring to it as "Louisiana Sappers and Miners." When the United States Army Adjutant General's Office was organizing the Confederate compiled military service records there was a lively debate amongst the clerks as to whether this was a Louisiana or a Confederate unit, the Confederate side finally winning out.[6]

Early in March 1861, Jules V. Gallimard of New Orleans visited President Davis in Montgomery and requested authority to organize a company of sappers, miners, and bombardiers for the regular army. According to Gallimard, this authority was granted and he returned to New Orleans and soon raised the company. Apparently Davis was thinking of the company authorized under the Act of March 6, but Gallimard was not commissioned in the regular Corps of Engineers and the War Department seems to have forgotten completely about him.[7]

---

[4] Warner, *Generals in Gray*, pp. 3-4, 28, 176-177, 179, 282-283, 292, 334-335.

[5] Nichols, *Confederate Engineers*, p. 92.

[6] Memo by E. K. Lundy, December 17, 1912, *CMSR*, Gallimard's Company Confederate Sappers and Bombardiers, RG 109, NA. Nichols, *Confederate Engineers*, pp. 91-92.

[7] Capt. J. V.Gallimard to Gen. G. G. Gorgas [sic]. January 26, 1863, Letters Received, A&IGO; Cooper to Capt. J. W. Frazer, April 24, 1861, and Cooper to Brig. Gen. A. R. Lawton, July 19, 1861, Letters Sent, A&IGO, Chap. I, Vol. 35, pp. 65, 273; RG 109, NA.

PRESIDENT JEFFERSON DAVIS
Courtesy of the Casement Museum.

From early May to December, Gallimard's Company spent most of its time in the swamps bordering Lake Borgne repairing and erecting fortifications under the direction of Major Martin L. Smith, at that time chief engineer of Department No. 1. Their efforts were at first expended at Battery Bienvenue, a small work built at the junction of Bayou Bienvenue and Bayou Mazant in 1826 and 1828 which blocked the route used by the British in 1815. The company also worked on Tower Dupre, a Martello tower erected at the mouth of Bayou Dupre in 1830. They returned to New Orleans Barracks on July 24. At that time, the company had a strength of five officers and ninety-two enlisted men. A detachment of five men under Second Lieutenant P. N. Judice accompanied Major Smith to Ship Island and worked on the fort there until its abandonment on September 16. Meanwhile, the remainder of the company had been ordered on August 8 to Proctorville on the shore of Lake Borgne, where they worked on an uncompleted tower fortification.[8]

The company returned to New Orleans on December 23 and was stationed at the New Marine Hospital. Under the orders of Major General Mansfield Lovell, the commander of Department No. 1, it helped to organize the hospital. In addition to this, the company provided details cleaning and repairing arms for Captain Richard Lambert at the Louisiana Arsenal. Major Smith apparently had to settle a dispute between Captains Gallimard and Lambert on how many of the men were to be used at the arsenal. Discipline appears to have been a growing problem. Three men deserted on January 27, 1862; seven on February 28; and seventeen March 11.[9]

The capture of Fort Donelson on the Tennessee River on February 16 quickly led to the collapse of the entire Confederate defense line in the West. Columbus, Kentucky, on the Mississippi River, was occupied by the Union fleet on March 4, forcing the Confederates to fall back to New Madrid, Missouri and Island No. 10 on the Kentucky-Tennessee state line. Thirty miles below Island No. 10, the Confederates began fortifying Fort Pillow on the first of the Chickasaw Bluffs on the Tennessee shore. Gallimard's Company was ordered to Fort Pillow from New Orleans in early March to join the command of Brigadier General John B. Villepigue. Villepigue immediately set the company to work erecting and equipping new batteries and powder magazines as he shortened the lines around the fort to make it more defensible for his small garrison. Island No. 10 fell to the combined Federal naval and land forces on April 7. The following day the Federal fleet chased the

---

[8] Dufour, *Night the War Was Lost*, p. 46. *OR*, Series I, Vol. LIII, p. 741. Post Returns, New Orleans Barracks, July and August 1861; Gallimard to Gorgas, January 26, 1863; RG 109, NA. The Proctorville fortified tower was not technically a Martello tower, but is commonly referred to as one.

[9] Gallimard to Lambert, January 9, 1862; Smith to Lambert, January 16, 1862; *CMSR*, Capt. J. V. Gallimard, Confederate Sappers and Miners, RG 109, NA.

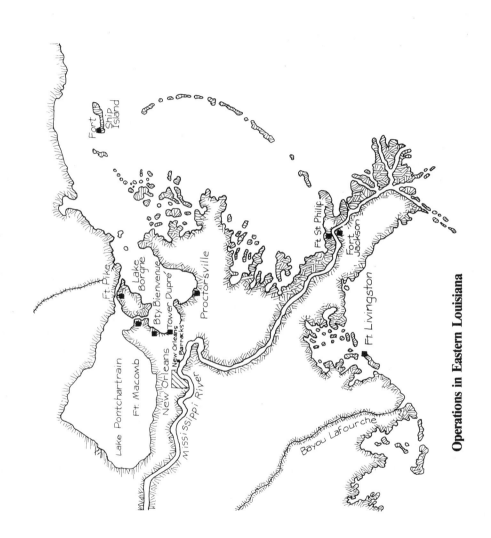

Operations in Eastern Louisiana

small Confederate river flotilla to Fort Pillow and received a few shots from the fort.

The following morning, the Union mortar boats were placed on the Arkansas side of the river under the protection of the gunboats and began firing on Fort Pillow. Plans to immediately attack the fort were frustrated by the withdrawal of most of the army force supporting the fleet. Attacks on the fort, therefore, were confined to mortar and long range firing. Gallimard's Company worked for fifty-three days under fire of the fleet attempting to strengthen the defenses. At the end of April, the company reported a strength of three officers and fifty-seven enlisted men. In addition to the deserters lost before its departure from New Orleans, two men had been discharged and First Lieutenant Charles de Lassus had deserted in Memphis on April 10. Surprisingly, discipline, instruction, and military appearance of the company were all reported to be good. On May 10, the eight rams of the Confederate River Defense Flotilla attacked the Union warships near Fort Pillow. In a fierce action, two Union gunboats and three of the rams were disabled before the Confederates withdrew. The Federals resumed the bombardment of Fort Pillow. General Beauregard determined on May 30 to abandon the fort and attempt to draw the enemy away from the river. On the night of June 4 Villepigue evacuated Fort Pillow, falling back to Grenada, Mississippi, with his troops.[10]

While the company was at Fort Pillow, General Villepigue had issued two orders in an attempt to raise recruits for the unit. The difficulty of getting properly qualified men transferred to the company and obtaining recruits in Memphis made these efforts ineffectual. When the company arrived in Grenada, it only had an aggregate strength of fifty officers and men. Gallimard's Company remained attached for the remainder of the summer to Villepique's command, which became the Second Brigade of Lovell's Division. This force was stationed along the Mississippi Central Railroad north of Grenada.

In early September, Major Generals Earl Van Dorn and Sterling Price began gathering forces to attempt to expel the Federals from West Tennessee. Van Dorn finally settled on attacking the Federal forces occupying Corinth. The Confederates found the bridges across the Hatchie River destroyed by the Federals. Gallimard with forty-seven men was put to work to replace the bridges, and in three and a half hours managed to erect a span 220 feet long which permitted the army to continue its advance. Following the

---

[10] *OR*, Series I, Vol. VII, p. 915; Vol. X, Part 1, pp. 902-903, and Part 2, pp. 394-396. Gallimard to Gorgas, January 26, 1863; Muster Roll, Gallimard's Company of Sappers and Miners, April 30, 1862; RG 109, NA. Mahan, *Gulf and Inland Waters*, pp. 39-40, 42-47; Scharf. *Confederate States Navy*, pp. 253-257.

disastrous repulse of Van Dorn's army at Corinth on October 3 and 4, Gallimard's Company, acting under the orders of General Lovell, moved out a day in advance of the retreating army and cut new roads through the thick woods covering the country and erected several bridges over the creeks and rivers. Villepigue was then transferred to command Port Hudson and requested Gallimard's Company, but was refused. The army remained briefly at Abbeville in November and then continued its retreat to the Grenada area. Gallimard's Company remained at Coffeeville and there apparently was a collapse of discipline as a result of the arduous and unsuccessful campaign. On December 8 at Coffeeville occurred the second mass desertion from the company during the war as eleven men took to the woods. Most of them were captured by the enemy, but three eventually rejoined the company.[11]

Gallimard reminded the War Department of the existence of the company in January 1863 when he asked to be allowed to fill his depleted ranks with conscripts. The company now only had three officers and thirty enlisted men. Colonel Josiah Gorgas, the Chief of Ordnance to whom the letter was erroneously addressed, stated in his endorsement that Gallimard's was the company organized under the Act of May 17, 1861. Colonel Gilmer pointed out that the company was formed in March 1861, and so could not be the May 17 one. This also seems clear from the fact that Gallimard had written that the company was to have as its main duty the instruction of officers and men in engineering duties, one of the provisions of the March 6 act.

Gallimard had energetically set to work in his spare time on this project and devised a course of eight classes for his men: fortifications; saps; mines; bridges and pontoons; military reconnaissance; and castramentation. He stated in his letter that they had mastered the first two and wanted to know if he should proceed with the rest of the schedule. Unfortunately, if any reply was made to this portion of the letter it has not survived.[12]

Finally aware of the existence of the company, the War Department decided to make it what its captain always thought it was. On October 24, 1863, the Engineer Bureau wrote Gallimard that he had been appointed a captain in the Corps of Engineers to command the Company of Sappers and Bombardiers under the Act of May 17, 1861. Since the act providing for the original engineer company specified that it would be commanded by one of the Corps of Engineers captains and all those vacancies were filled, it appears that Gallimard was appointed under the second act because that was

---

[11] *OR*, Series I, Vol. X, Part 2, p. 608; Vol. XVII, Part 1, pp. 379, 404, and Part 2, pp. 600, 661. Hartje, *Van Dorn*, p. 219. Gallimard to Gorgas, January 26, 1863, *loc. cit.*

[12] Muster Roll, Gallimard's Company of Sappers and Miners, December 31, 1862; Gallimard to Gorgas, January 26, 1863; RG 109, NA.

the only vacancy in the grade of captain. It is interesting that in October 1863 the company muster rolls stop being made out as Sappers and Miners and become Sappers and Bombardiers. The names of the lieutenants appearing on the company muster rolls in the War Department differed from those in an order of Major Martin L. Smith. The appointments of the lieutenants were held up awaiting an explanation of this discrepancy and were never made.[13]

While the War Department was finally legalizing the existence of the company, events were taking place in Mississippi. Following the retreat from Abbeville, the company for several months was nearly idle. Sometime in the spring of 1863, Gallimard's Company was transferred south. On the morning of April 17, Colonel Benjamin H. Grierson and 1,700 Union cavalrymen marched out of LaGrange, Tennessee, and began one of the most spectacular raids of the war. Destroying railroads and supply bases, Grierson created consternation in the Confederate rear areas as he marched south through Mississippi. As hastily gathered Confederate forces converged, Grierson threatened Magnolia and Osyka. Colonel W. R. Miles' Louisiana Legion had been ordered from Port Hudson to Clinton, and was then directed toward Osyka to intercept the raiders. Miles apparently picked up Gallimard's Company at Clinton and early on the morning of May 1 reached the Amite River. The water of the river and adjoining swamp was high and it took Gallimard five hours to construct a temporary bridge to allow the passage of the artillery and trains. By that time it was too late. Grierson had fought a skirmish at the Tickfaw River and then moved off toward Baton Rouge. Miles was ordered to proceed with his command to protect the Confederate supplies at Osyka. Gallimard's Company remained in the area between Clinton and Osyka until late July repairing roads. The only excitement seems to have been on July 13 when jumpy Confederate pickets shot and killed the captain's horse near Osyka.[14]

About July 26, 1863, Gallimard's Company was transferred from Mississippi to Mobile. This move must have pleased its commander as he had been urging that the company would be better employed working on fortifications. When it arrived in Mobile is not known, as it first appears on a troop list of the Department of the Gulf on September 13.[15]

---

[13] James A. Seddon to President Davis, February 5, 1864, Letters Sent, Secretary of War, Chap. IX, Vol. 99, p. 121; Lt. Col. A. L. Rives to Gallimard, October 24, 1863, Letters Sent, Engineer Bureau, Chap. III, Vol. 4, p. 45; RG 109, NA. The remark's about the company's lieutenants are on the back of an endorsement dated October 13, 1863, in *CMSR*, Col. R. R. Garland, 6th Texas Infantry, RG 109, NA.

[14] *OR*, Series I, Vol. XXIV, Part 1, p. 545. Gallimard to H. Taylor, 2d Auditor, War Department, August 20, 1863, *CMSR*, Capt. J. V. Gallimard, Confederate Sappers and Miners, RG 109, NA.

[15] Lt. Col. V. Sheliha to Col. S. H. Lockett, December 10, 1864, Letters Sent, Engineer Office, District of the Gulf, Chap. III, Vol. 13, pp. 225-227, RG 109, NA. *OR*, Series I, Vol. XXVI, Part 2, pp. 275, 403.

On December 2, First Lieutenant Charles Armand Brisset was ordered to proceed to Pollard, Alabama, and to report to Brigadier General James H. Clanton for the erection of a palisade to defend the Mobile and Gulf Railroad northeast of Mobile. At the end of the year, the company could still muster only three officers and thirty-two enlisted men. After its arrival in Mobile, attempts had been made to fill its ranks, but many of the men were of poor quality. Discipline was good, but the company had no muskets since the retreat from Corinth. Its accoutrements were in very bad order and entirely unfit, the clothing was insufficient, and the men were without blankets.[16]

On March 7, 1864, Captain Gallimard was temporarily detached from the company and placed on duty as engineer in charge of the lower bay lines of the defenses of Mobile. He was never to return to the company. First Lieutenant Jacques Emile Bel assumed command of the company. Gallimard's first assignment was to superintend the construction of fortifications on Dauphin Island on the west side of the entrance to Mobile Bay and to put in place the channel obstructions.[17]

Brisset and the men with him were ordered back to Mobile from Pollard on April 16. Lieutenant Colonel Victor von Sheliha, the chief engineer of the District of the Gulf, agreed with Gallimard that Sughee Point on Little Dauphin Island was a key position in the western part of the lower bay line, but work was delayed because of a shortage of laborers and transportation. Work had to be deferred until completion of the new redoubt east of Fort Morgan on the opposite side of the bay mouth.[18]

On June 15, Brisset was ordered back to Pollard with an overseer, a gang of fifteen slaves, rations for fifteen days, and a 2-mule wagon. Detachments of the company were employed at both Fort Gaines on Dauphin Island and Fort Powell on the western side of the bay. On August 3, Union troops under Major General Gordon Granger landed on the west end of Dauphin Island and invested Fort Gaines. The Union fleet under Admiral Farragut forced the entrance of Mobile Bay on August 5 in a spectacular battle with the forts and a small Confederate Navy squadron. Fort Gaines and Fort Powell fell on August 9 and most of the Union force was shifted to Mobile Point to begin the siege of Fort Morgan. A severe bombardment from all directions once the Union fleet was in the bay reduced the massive

---

[16] Sheliha to Brisset, December 2, 1863, *CMSR,* Charles Armand Brisset, Confederate Sappers and Miners; Muster Roll, Gallimard's Company of Sappers and Bombardiers, December 31, 1863; RG 109, NA. *OR,* Series I, Vol. XXVI, Part 2, pp. 511, 562.

[17] Special Order No. 6, Letters Sent, Engineer Office, District of the Gulf, Chap. III, Vol. 12, p. 643, RG 109, NA. *OR,* Series I, Vol. XXXII, Part 3, p. 578.

[18] Sheliha to Brisset, April 16, 1864, Letters Sent, Engineer Office, District of the Gulf, Chap. III, Vol. 12, p. 642, RG 109, NA. *OR,* Series I, Vol. XXXII, Part 3, p. 810.

brick fort to a wreck. On August 23, Brigadier General Richard L. Page finally surrendered to avoid further loss of life. Gallimard had been the engineer in charge of the fort during the siege and was commended by his commander. Following the surrender, Gallimard was sent to Fort Warren in Boston Harbor and remained a prisoner of war until his release on taking the oath of allegiance on June 12, 1865.[19]

The capture of the forts at the mouth of Mobile Bay did not lead to the immediate fall of the port city. Von Sheliha had constructed a strong series of inner fortifications and the Federals did not have the force available to overcome these defenses. Bel remained in command of what was left of the company and Brisset appears to have been on detached duty. The company had roll call in its quarters at 8:30 p.m. each night, and all the men were required to be present. The Chief of the Engineer Bureau had determined that any duty engineer troops were required to do was legitimate and there was no extra duty. By November 1, there were only two officers and eight men left in the company. Von Sheliha recommended that the remains of the company be consolidated with the 2d Confederate Engineer Regiment. This Provisional Army organization consisted of widely scattered companies in Mobile, Charleston, Savannah, and Wilmington. Von Sheliha commended the zeal and efficiency of Brisset and recommended that he be promoted to captain of one of the regiment's companies, but had nothing good to say about Bel and proposed that he be transferred to some other command.[20]

On December 14, Brisset went to Richmond with the accounts of the engineers of the District of the Gulf and the Department of Alabama, Mississippi, and East Louisiana. He reported to General Gilmer and then returned to Mobile. Apparently the remains of Gallimard's Company were consolidated with Company A, 2d Confederate Engineer Regiment, probably commanded by First Lieutenant S. McD. Vernon. In the spring of 1865, the Federals finally had sufficient troops available to complete the capture of Mobile. On April 8 they forced the evacuation of Spanish Fort on the east side of the upper bay and carried Fort Blakely by assault the following day. With the defense line breached, Major General Dabney H. Maury had no choice but to evacuate the city on the night of April 11, removing what supplies he could and burning the stocks of cotton. Maury's troops reached Meridian, Mississippi, without opposition and began refitting with the hope of

[19] Sheliha to Brisset, June 15, 1864, *CMSR*, Charles Armand Brisset, Confederate Sappers and Miners; *CMSR*, Capt. J. V. Gallimard, Confederate Sappers and Miners; RG 109, NA. *OR*, Series I, Vol. XXXIX, Part 1, p. 441. There is a map of the lower bay defenses by Gallimard in *OR*, Atlas, Plate LXIII-6.

[20] Sheliha to Bel, September 6, 1864, Letters Sent, Engineer Office, District of the Gulf, Chap. III, Vol. 13, p. 28; Sheliha to Lockett, December 10, 1864, *loc. cit.;* RG109, NA. Nichols, *Confederate Engineers*, p. 94. *OR*, Series I, Vol. XXXIX, Part 3, p. 877.

joining the Army of Tennessee. From Meridian on April 24, Colonel Samuel H. Lockett, chief engineer of the department, ordered Brisset to take Vernon's company and proceed to Gainesville, Alabama, with a work gang of 100 slaves. The end had come, however. On May 4 at Citronelle, forty miles north of Mobile, Lieutenant General Richard Taylor surrendered the Confederate forces in the Department of Alabama, Mississippi, and East Louisiana. When Company A, 2d Confederate Engineers, was paroled at Gainesville on May 10 there were only Brisset and three enlisted men of Gallimard's Company left. Interestingly, two of these men had been captured at Fort Gaines, exchanged in January 1865, and rejoined the company.[21]

The service of Gallimard's Company, at least until its transfer to Mobile, seems to have been on the whole satisfactory and was commended on occasion. Its captain did his best to make it a highly trained unit, but the realities of hard campaigning tended to thwart his efforts. After its arrival in Mobile attempts to bring the company up to strength were unsuccessful and it was employed mostly in small detachments while Gallimard and Brisset spent most of their time on detached service. Records for six officers and ninety-nine enlisted men who served with the company have been found, but the scarcity of muster rolls prevents a complete assessment of all the enlisted men assigned during the war. From the surviving records it appears that the company had 1 officer and 11 men captured, 8 of the men eventually rejoining the Confederates and 3 joining the Union Army. One officer and thirty-four enlisted men deserted, most of them on March 11, 1862, at New Orleans and on December 8, 1862, at Coffeeville. One officer and four men were paroled at the end of the war while still in service. Two died in service, 2 were discharged, and there is no record of what finally happened to 1 officer and 42 men. Both Brisset and Bel had been promoted from the ranks in 1862. It had been a hard war for an unusual unit.

---

[21] Sheliha to Brisset, December 14, 1864, and Lockett to Brisset, April 24, 1865, *CMSR,* Charles Armand Brisset, Confederate Sappers and Miners; *CMSR,* Confederate Sappers and Miners; RG 109, NA. *OR,* Series I, Vol. XLIX, Part 1, pp. 1045-1046.

Chapter VII

RETROSPECT

The Confederate regular army, just as the United States regular army, proved to be of virtually no tactical significance during the Civil War. Starting from scratch, the Confederates only were able to organize a small fraction of the regular units authorized by law. With an authorized strength of over 15,000, the Confederates were only able to raise a regular force of about 1,650, and half of these were officers. In contrast, the United States started the war with a small, but relatively intact, organization consisting of ten regiments of infantry, five of cavalry, and four of artillery. In the early months of the war the regular army was expanded, at least on paper, to nineteen infantry regiments, six of cavalry, and five of artillery and added about 25,000 men to the authorized strength. But for reasons similar to those that aborted recruiting the Confederate regulars, the United States regulars were never brought up to full strength and served with few exceptions in scattered fragments throughout the field armies. By the end of the war, most United States regular units were so reduced in strength that they were withdrawn to forts in the North for reorganization and recruitment. If the United States regulars had been recruited to full strength during the war, they would have numbered 44,893, but the most men they ever had was 25,480 in June 1862.[1]

---

[1] Heitman, *Historical Register*, Vol. II, pp. 598-601, 626.

The impact of the regulars on both sides, however, was far out of proportion to their numbers and was most evident in the service of regular officers with volunteer units. Emory Upton later was to write that the logical thing for the Union to have done was to break up the regular army at the beginning of the war and disperse its trained officers and men as cadre for the new volunteer units.[2] This was not done, and although most of the regular officers eventually did hold volunteer commissions, most of the volunteer units did not have the advantage of experienced officers and noncommissioned officers to begin with. The Confederates actually came much closer to Upton's concept, but not by plan. The failure to recruit more than a handful of companies meant that the regular officer corps, which was brought completely up to strength except for lieutenants, did become dispersed throughout the volunteer force. As previously noted, since many of the officers did not hold state commissions they tended to fill a significant portion of the staff positions.

The story of the Confederate regulars has remained shrouded in ignorance and misunderstanding since the Civil War. First, this was a result of the evident confusion of the Confederate War Department regarding these units late in the war. The War Department on several occasions obviously had trouble remembering the few regular units that existed. Second, the so-called state regulars caused confusion at the time and ever since as to what were "regular" units. And finally, there seems to have been an almost deliberate policy on the part of the United States War Department after it came into possession of the Confederate War Department records not to admit that there had been a Confederate regular army.

A discussion of the regular officers who served with volunteer units in the Provisional Army of the Confederate States is far beyond the scope of this study. Some idea of the impact of the regular officers may be found in the previous chapters. Of the units themselves, however, it is possible to come to some conclusions. Regular units like units in almost all armies at all time were as good as the officers who led them. This truism is best illustrated by the 1st Confederate Light Artillery Battery. Under Oliver Semmes and his capable young West Point officers the unit was one of the finest light artillery batteries in the Confederate Army. This was true even though it was formed from the same material as the other companies of the Infantry School of Practice which behaved miserably after the fall of the New Orleans forts. Other units containing regulars, such as the batteries of the 1st Louisiana Heavy Artillery, also reflected that quality until decimated and worn out by hard campaigning. Company A, 1st Confederate Regular

---

[2] Upton, *Military Policy*, pp. 235-238.

Cavalry, when led by Ingraham and Bradley, was a good unit, but disintegrated when Denys, its last officer, deserted during the Nashville Campaign. Under Hayne's leadership Company C, 15th South Carolina Heavy Artillery Battalion, had a commendable record throughout the war, with the exception of 1864 when the Marylanders in the unit wanted to be transferred nearer home after their regular enlistments expired.

With the exception of Semmes' battery and perhaps Hayne's company, the inability to keep the regular units up to strength sapped their effectiveness. Both of these units received infusions of conscripts and remained viable organizations to the end. Gallimard's Company of Sappers and Bombardiers did excellent service until it was unable to replace the losses suffered during the Corinth Campaign with recruits or conscripts. Company A, 1st Confederate Regular Cavalry, slowly melted away until the final disaster in Tennessee. The remaining regular units were so small and scattered that no real assessment can be made of them.

The enlisted men of the Confederate regular army appear from the surviving records to be very similar to those composing the regular army of the United States. There was a high percentage of foreign born, the majority probably were unskilled, there was a significant leavening of professional soldiers, and there may well have been more of an attachment to the unit and its commander than to the cause of Southern independence. The latter was certainly true of the cavalry company and probably also of Semmes' battery. Emory Upton's assertion that only twenty-six United States regular enlisted men joined the Confederates has been repeated many times by historians. Records of over seventy former United States regulars, however, have been identified in the Confederate regular army and there probably were more. As many as 400 former United States enlisted men may have served altogether in the Confederate Army. Unfortunately the fragmentary nature of the original personnel records will make it impossible to ever obtain a completely accurate statistical assessment of the enlisted men.

Unrecognized at the time, unremembered since, the Confederate regulars are still a part of the history of the Lost Cause. Tiny though it was, the regular army was present in every theater of operations during the war and upheld the traditions of the American professional soldier. Only a footnote in history, the Confederate regular army still deserves to be remembered.

Bibliography

This account of the Confederate regular army is mainly based on original documents in the National Archives. Records relating to the regulars are widely scattered and contained in many record groups. The following record groups were consulted:

War Department Collection of Confederate Records, Record Group 109.
Records of The Adjutant General's Office, Record Group 94.
Records of United States Army Commands, Record Group 98.
Records of the Office of the Secretary of War, Record Group 107.
Records of the Office of the Commissary General of Prisoners, Record Group 249.
Records of the Veterans Administration, Record Group 15.

The following books and articles were also used in the preparation of this account:

Barr, Alwyn. "Confederate Artillery in the Trans-Mississippi," *Military Affairs*, Vol. XXVII, No. 2 (Summer 1963), pp. 77-83.

_____. "Confederate Artillery in Western Louisiana, 1862-1863," *Civil War History*, Vol. 9, No. 1 (March 1963), pp. 74-85.

Bergeron, Arthur W., Jr. *Guide to Louisiana Confederate Military Units, 1861-1865*. Baton Rouge: Louisiana State University Press, 1989.

Brown, D. Alexander. *The Galvanized Yankees*. Urbana: University of Illinois Press, 1963.

Burton, E. Milby. *The Siege of Charleston, 1861-1865*. Columbia: University of South Carolina Press, 1970.

Casey, Powell A. *Encyclopedia of Forts, Posts, Named Camps and Other Military Installations in Louisiana, 1700-1981*. Baton Rouge: Claitor's Publishing Division, 1983.

Cassidy, Vincent H. and Simpson, Amos E. *Henry Watkins Allen of Louisiana*. Baton Rouge: Louisiana State University Press, 1964.

Chesnut, Mary Boykin. *A Diary From Dixie*. Boston: Houghton Mifflin Co., 1949.

Coffman, Edward M. *The Old Army, A Portrait of the American Army in Peacetime, 1784-1898.* New York and Oxford: Oxford University Press, 1986.

Confederate States of America, Congress. *Journal of the Congress of the Confederate States of America, 1861-1865*, 7 vols. Senate Document No. 234, 2nd Session, 58th Congress.

_____. *Statutes at Large of the Provisional Government of the Confederate States of America.* Richmond: R. M. Smith, Printer to Congress, 1864.

Confederate States of America, War Department. *Army Regulations, 1862.* Richmond: J. W. Randolph, 1862.

Davis, William C. *The Orphan Brigade; the Kentucky Confederates Who Couldn't Go Home.* Baton Rouge: Louisiana State University Press, 1980.

DeLeon, Thomas Cooper. *Four Years in Rebel Capitals.* Mobile: The Gossip Printing Co., 1890.

Dufour, Charles L. *The Night the War Was Lost.* Garden City: Doubleday & Co., Inc., 1960.

Dyer, John P. *From Shiloh to San Juan.* Baton Rouge: Louisiana State University of Press, 1961.

_____. *The Gallant Hood.* Indianapolis and New York: The Bobbs-Merrill Co., Inc., 1950.

Fay, Edwin H. *This Infernal War.* Austin: University of Texas Press, 1958.

Frazer, Robert W. *Forts of the West.* Norman: University of Oklahoma Press, 1965.

Freeman, Douglas S. *R. E. Lee, A Biography*, 4 vols. New York and London: Charles Scribner's Sons, 1934.

Hall, Martin Hardwick. *Sibley's New Mexico Campaign.* Austin: University of Texas Press, 1960.

Hamersly, Thomas H. S. *Complete General Navy Register of the United States of America from 1776 to 1887.* New York: T. H. S. Hamersly, 1888.

Harding, George C. *The Miscellaneous Writings of George C. Harding.* Indianapolis: Carlon & Hollenbeck, 1882.

Hart, Herbert M. *Old Forts of the Southwest.* New York: Bonanza Books, 1964.

Hartje, Robert G. *Van Dorn: The Life and Times of a Confederate General.* Nashville: Vanderbilt University Press, 1967.

Hassler, Warren W. (ed.) *The General to His Lady.* Chapel Hill: University of North Carolina Press, 1962.

Hattaway, Herman. *General Stephen D. Lee.* Jackson: University Press of Mississippi, 1976.

Hay, Thomas Robson. "Lucius Northrop: Commissary General of the Confederacy," *Civil War History*, Vol. VI (May 1963), pp. 5-23.

Heitman, Francis B. *Historical Register and Dictionary of The United States Army*, 2 vols. Washington: Government Printing Office, 1903.

Henry, Robert S. *"First With the Most" Forrest.* Indianapolis and New York: Bobbs-Merrill Co., 1944.

Hughes, Nathaniel Cheairs, Jr. *General William J. Hardee: Old Reliable.* Baton Rouge: Louisiana State University Press, 1965.

Johnson, John. *The Defense of Charleston Harbor.* Charleston: Walker, Evans & Cogswell Co., 1890.

Jones, John B. *A Rebel War Clerk's Diary*, 2 vols. Philadelphia: J. B. Lippincott Co., 1866.

Jones, Terry L. *Lee's Tigers: The Louisiana Infantry in the Army of the Potomac*, Baton Rouge: Louisiana State University Press, 1987.

Kreidberg, Marvin A. and Henry, Merton G. *History of Military Mobilization in the United States Army, 1775-1945.* Washington: Department of the Army Pamphlet No. 20-212, 1955.

Lester, W. W. and Bromwell, William J. *A Digest of the Military and Naval Laws of the Confederate States.* Columbia: Evans and Cogswell, 1864.

Lewis, Kenneth E. and Langhorne, William T., Jr. *Castle Pinckney: An Archaelogical Assessment and Recommendations.* Columbia: Institute for Archeology and Anthropology, University of South Carolina, 1978.

Long, E. B. *The Civil War Day by Day.* Garden City: Doubleday & Co., Inc., 1971.

Lonn, Ella. *Foreigners in the Union Army and Navy.* Baton Rouge: Louisiana State University Press, 1952.

Lossing, Benson J. *Pictorial History of the Civil War.* Philadelphia: David McKay, 1866.

Mahan, Alfred T. *The Gulf and Inland Waters.* New York: The Blue & Gray Press, n.d.

Morelock, Jerry D. "Ride to the River of Death: Cavalry Operations in the Chickamauga Campaign," *Military Review*, Vol. LXIV, No. 10 (October 1984), pp. 2-20.

Nichols, James L. *Confederate Engineers*. Tuscaloosa: Confederate Publishing Co., Inc., 1957.

Oates, Stephen B. *Confederate Cavalry West of the River*. Austin: University of Texas Press, 1961.

Outline Descriptions of the Posts of the Military Division of the Missouri. Fort Collins, Colo.: Old Army Press, 1972.

Owen, Thomas W. *History of Alabama and Dictionary of Alabama Biography*, 4 vols. Chicago: S. J. Clarke Publishing Co., 1921.

Parks, Joseph H. *General E. Kirby Smith, C.S.A.* Baton Rouge: Louisiana State University Press, 1954.

Parsons, W. H. (Bryce Suderow, ed.). ' "The World Never Witnessed Such Fights,' " *Civil War Times Illustrated*, Vol. XXIV, No. 5 (September 1985), pp. 20-25.

Patrick, Rembert W. (ed.). *The Opinions of the Confederate Attorney General, 1861-1865*. Buffalo: Denis & Co., Inc., 1950.

Price, Marshall Moore. *Conquest of a Valley*. Charlottesville: The University Press of Virginia, 1965.

Richardson, James D. (ed.). *A Compilation of the Messages and Papers of the Confederacy*, 2 vols. Nashville, 1906.

Ripley, Warren (ed.). *Siege Train, the Journals of a Confederate Artilleryman in the Defense of Charleston*. Columbia: University of South Carolina Press, 1986.

Robinson, William M. "The Confederate Engineers," *Military Engineer*, Vol. XXII (1930), pp. 297-305, 410-419, 512-517.

Scharf, Thomas. *History of the Confederate Navy*. New York: The Fairfax Press, n.d.

Semmes, Maj. O. J. "First Confederate Battery An Orphan," *Confederate Veteran*, Vol. XXI (1913), p. 58.

Sheppard, Eric William. *Bedford Forrest: The Confederacy's Greatest Cavalryman*. London: H. F. & G. Witherby, 1930.

Squires, Charles W. " 'My Artillery Fire Was Very Destructive,' " *Civil War Times Illustrated*, Vol. XIV, No. 3 (June 1975), pp. 18-16.

Taylor, Richard. *Destruction and Reconstruction*. New York: Longman, Green and Co., 1955.

Todd, Frederick P. *American Military Equipage, 1851-1872*. New York: Charles Scribner's Sons, 1980.

United States Department of the Army. *The Army Lineage Book*, Vol. II, *Infantry*, Washington: Government Printing Office, 1953.

United States Navy Department. *Dictionary of American Naval Fighting Ships*, 8 vols. Washington: Naval History Division, 1959-1981.

_____. *Official Records of the Union and Confederate Navies in the War of the Rebellion*, 26 vols. Washington: Government Printing Office, 1894-1922.

United States War Department. *Army Register, 1861*. Washington: The Adjutant General's Office, 1861.

_____. *List of Artillery Officers and Organizations of the Confederate States Army, 1861-1865*. Washington, n.d.

_____. *List of Field Officers, Regiments and Battalions of the Confederate States Army, 1861-1865*. Washington, n.d.

_____. *List of Staff Officers, Confederate States Army, 1861-1865*. Washington, n.d.

_____. *War of the Rebellion: A Compilation of the Official Records of the Union and Confederate Armies*. 130 vols. Washington: Government Printing Office, 1880-1901.

Upton, Emory. *The Military Policy of the United States*. Washington: War Department, Office of the Chief of Staff, 1912.

Warner, Ezra J. *Generals in Blue*. Baton Rouge: Louisiana State University Press, 1964.

_____. *Generals in Gray*. Baton Rouge: Louisiana State University Press, 1959.

Weinert, Richard P. "The Confederate Regular Cavalry," *Texana*. Vol. X, No. 3 (1972), pp. 244-259.

_____. "The Confederate Regulars in Louisiana," *Louisiana Studies*, Vol. VI, No. 1 (Spring 1967), pp. 53-71.

_____. "The Neglected Key to the Gulf of Mexico," *The Journal of Mississippi History*, Vol. XXXI, No. 4 (November 1969), pp. 269-301.

Appendix A

LIST OF
REGULAR ARMY OFFICERS

The first rank shown is the Confederate regular army rank. The rank in parenthesis is the highest rank of any type attained during the war. A * indicates killed in battle or died of wounds.

Adams, Capt. John (Brig. Gen.)*
Adams, 2d Lt. Samuel F.
Adams, Capt. Soloman
Alexander, Capt. Edward Porter (Brig. Gen.)
Alexander, 2d Lt. John A.
Alexander, 2d Lt. Joseph A.
Alexander, Cadet L. A.
Alexander, 2d Lt. T. Bullitt
Alexander, Cadet W. K.
Alston, 1st Lt. Benjamin (Col.)
Anderson, 1st Lt. Charles D. (Col.)
Anderson, 2d Lt. Edward Willoughby (Capt.)
Anderson, Maj. Richard Herron (Lt. Gen.)
Anderson, 1st Lt. Robert Houstoun
   (Brig. Gen.)
Anderson, Lt. Col. Samuel Smith
Anderson, Surg. William Wallace
Andrews, 2d Lt. Garnett, Jr. (Lt. Col.)
Ansley, 1st Lt. John Urquhart (Capt.)
Archer, Capt. James Jay (Brig. Gen.)
Archer, 1st Lt. James W. (Capt.)
Archer, Capt. John
Archer, 2d Lt. William S.
Armistead, 1st Lt. Franck S. (Col.)
Armistead, Maj. Lewis Addison (Brig. Gen.)*
Armstrong, 2d Lt. Frank C. (Brig. Gen.)
Ashe, 2d Lt. John Grange (Capt.)
Ashe, 2d Lt. Samuel A. (Capt.)
Atkinson, 2d Lt. R. W.
Ayer, Cadet Alfred A.

Bagley, 1st Lt. Edward F. (Maj.)*
Bagwell, 1st Lt. George H. (Capt.)
Baldwin, 1st Lt. Briscoe G., Jr. (Lt. Col.)
Baldwin, Capt. William Edwin (Brig. Gen.)
Balfour, 1st Lt. Joseph D. (Maj.)*
Ball, 2d Lt. Charles P. (Col.)
Ball, Capt. Glover A. (Maj.)
Baltzell, 2d Lt. James P. (Capt.)
Barksdale, Cadet Harris (2d Lt.)
Barnes, 2d Lt. John T. Mason (Capt.)
Barnett, Cadet William H.
Barnwell, 1st Lt. William F.

Barrow, 2d Lt. James (Lt. Col.)*
Barton, Cadet R. L.
Beall, Capt. Seth Maxwell (Brig. Gen.)
Beall, Capt. William Nelson Rector
   (Brig. Gen.)
Beauregard, Cadet Henri T.
Beauregard, Gen. Pierre Gustave Toutant
Beauregard, 2d Lt. Rene T. (Maj.)
Bechter, 2d Lt. M. Herman A.
Beckham, 1st Lt. Robert F. (Col.)*
Bee, Maj. Barnard Elliott (Brig. Gen.)*
Berney, 2d Lt. John S.
Berrien, Asst. Surg. James H.
Berrien, 2d Lt. James McPherson (1st Lt.)
Berry, 1st Lt. Thomas J. (Lt. Col.)
Blair, Maj. William B. (Col.)
Blake, Capt. Edward D. (Lt. Col.)
Blakistone, 2d Lt. William T.
Blocker, 2d Lt. John Rufus (Maj.)
Blount, 2d Lt. Joseph Guy (Maj.)
Blow, 2d Lt. Henry L. (1st Lt.)
Boatwright, 2d Lt. John L. (Capt.)
Boggs, Capt. William R. (Brig. Gen.)
Bolton, 1st Lt. Henry (Capt.)
Bonneau, Capt. Richard Vanderhost (Maj.)
Bonner, 2d Lt. William G. (Maj.)
Booker, 2d Lt. Richard Marshall (Capt.)
Booth, Capt. John C. (Maj.)
Borland, 2d Lt. Harold (Maj.)
Boteler, 2d Lt. Alexander R., Jr.
Bowles, 2d Lt. James W. (Lt. Col.)
Bradford, 1st Lt. Jefferson Davis (Maj.)
Bradford, 2d Lt. William K. (Capt.)
Bradfute, Capt. William R. (Col.)
Bradley, 2d Lt. John (Capt.)
Bragg, Gen. Braxton
Branch, 1st Lt. John L.*
Brand, Cadet George C.
Brewer, Asst. Surg. Charles
Brewer, 1st Lt. Richard H. (Col.)*
Brice, 1st Lt. Jacob (Capt.)
Brickell, 2d Lt. William W.
Brodie, Asst. Surg. Robert Little

Brown, 2d Lt. Charles H. (Capt.)
Brown, Cadet Charles M.
Brown, Capt. John A. (Col.)
Brown, Cadet Richard L., Jr.
Brown, Maj. William Leroy (Lt. Col.)
Bruton, 2d Lt. Thomas J. (1st Lt.)
Bryan, 2d Lt. Henry (Maj.)
Bryan, 2d Lt. James A. (Capt.)
Bryant, 2d Lt. John C. Herbert (Capt.)
Bullock, 2d Lt. Waller R. (1st Lt.)
Burkhart, Capt. Philip
Burnet, 1st Lt. William E. (Col.)
Burnwell, Cadet N. B.
Burton, Maj. James H.
Burtwell, 1st Lt. John R. B. (Col.)
Burwell, 2d Lt. Philip L. (Capt.)
Bush, 2d Lt. Thomas (Capt.)*
Butler, 2d Lt. Lawrence L. (Maj.)
Butler, 2d Lt. Lee M. (Capt.)
Butler, 1st Lt. William (Col.)

Cabell, Maj. William Lewis (Brig. Gen.)
Calhoun, Maj. J. Lawrence
Callahan, 2d Lt. Dennis (Capt.)
Campbell, 2d Lt. Charles Carroll (Maj.)
Carr, Capt. George Watson (Lt. Col.)
Causey, 2d Lt. Charles H. (Capt.)
Chambers, 2d Lt. Robert A. (Capt.)
Chambliss, 2d Lt. Nathaniel Rives (Maj.)
Chapman, Cadet William Henry
Chestney, 2d Lt. Theodore O. (Maj.)
Childs, Capt. Frederick L. (Lt. Col.)
Chilton, Col. Robert Hall (Brig. Gen.)
Christian, Cadet Richard M.
Claiborne, Maj. Thomas, Jr.
Clark, Cadet S. Churchill (Capt.)*
Clarke, 2d Lt. John J. (Col.)
Clarke, Capt. William J. (Col.)
Clay, Lt. Col. Hugh Lawson
Clay, 2d Lt. Thomas J. (Maj.)
Clayton, 2d Lt. Arthur
Clayton, 2d Lt. George Wesley (Col.)
Cobb, Cadet James H.
Cole, Capt. Robert Granderson (Lt. Col.)
Collins, Capt. Charles Read (Col.)*
Collins, Cadet James A.
Cone, 1st Lt. Aurelius F. (Lt. Col.)
Cook, Cadet E. S.

Cooke, 1st Lt. John Rogers (Brig. Gen.)
Cooper, 2d Lt. John W.
Cooper, Gen. Samuel
Cooper, 1st Lt. Samuel M. (Maj.)
Corley, Maj. James L. (Lt. Col.)
Covey, Asst. Surg. Edward N.
Cowan, 2d Lt. James G. (Capt.)
Craige, Cadet James A.
Crittenden, Col. George Bibb (Maj. Gen.)
Cross, Capt. Alexander H.
Crowell, Asst. Surg. Nathanial Savage
Culbertson, 1st Lt. Jacob (Capt.)
Cumming, Maj. Alfred (Brig. Gen.)
Cunningham, 1st Lt. Arthur S. (Lt. Col.)
Cunningham, 1st Lt. Edward (Maj.)
Cunningham, 1st Lt. George A. (Col.)
Cutshaw, 2d Lt. Wilfred E. (Lt. Col.)
Cuyler, Capt. Richard M. (Lt. Col.)

Dabney, 2d Lt. Edward (Capt.)*
Dancy, 2d Lt. Robert F.*
Dandridge, 2d Lt. Philip P.
Dangerfield, Capt. J. E. P.
Dargan, Cadet Edmund P.
Davis, Capt. Matthew L., Jr. (Col.)
Deane, Cadet F. H., Jr.
Dearing, 2d Lt. James (Brig. Gen.)*
Dearing, 2d Lt. St. Clair (Lt. Col.)
Deas, Lt. Col. George
Deas, 2d Lt. William A. (Capt.)
De Lagnel, Capt. Julius Adolphus
    (Lt. Col.)
De Leon, Surg. David Camden
Dent, Cadet Stevens T.
Denys, 2d Lt. John H.
Derrick, 2d Lt. Clarence (Lt. Col.)
DeSaussure, Capt. Willam Davis (Col.)*
Deshler, Capt. James (Brig. Gen.)*
Dickens, 2d Lt. John Hemphill
Dickenson, Cadet Jesse J.
Dillon, 1st Lt. Edward (Col.)
Dixon, 1st Lt. Joseph (Capt.)*
Dixon, 2d Lt. Joseph Koger (Maj.)
Dobbin, 2d Lt. James C., Jr.
Donelson, Cadet Samuel (2d Lt.)
Doswell, Cadet Grey
Downer, Maj. W. S.
Drinkard, Capt. W. F.

DuBarry, 2d Lt. Franklin B. (Capt.)
DuBose, 1st Lt. Dudley McIver (Brig. Gen.)
Duncan, Capt. Johnson Kelly (Brig. Gen.)
Dunlap, 2d Lt. William Watkins (Maj.)
Duval, 2d Lt. Harvie Sheffield

Echols, Capt. William Holding (Maj.)
Edelin, 1st Lt. Thomas Boyd (Lt. Col.)
Edwards, 1st Lt. O. W. (Capt.)
Ellis, 1st Lt. Towson (Maj.)
Ellis, Cadet William A.
Elzey, Lt. Col. Arnold (Maj. Gen.)
Emack, 2d Lt. George M. (Maj.)
Evans, Capt. Nathan George (Brig. Gen.)
Ewell, Lt. Col. Richard Stoddert (Lt. Gen.)

Faison, 2d Lt. Paul F. (Col.)
Farish, 2d Lt. W. S.
Farley, 2d Lt. Henry S. (Maj.)
Faulkner, 1st Lt. Sanford C. (Capt.)
Fauntleroy, Asst. Surg. Archibald McGill
Fauntleroy, 2d Lt. Thomas K. (Capt.)
Ferguson, 1st Lt. Samuel Wragg (Brig. Gen.)
Field, Capt. Charles William (Maj. Gen.)
Finney, 1st Lt. Newton S. (Capt.)
Foard, Surg. Andrew Jackson
Fogg, Cadet William G.
Foote, 2d Lt. Henry S., Jr. (1st Lt.)
Forney, Capt. John Horace (Maj. Gen.)
Forsberg, 1st Lt. August (Col.)
Forsyth, 2d Lt. Charles A.
Frazer, Capt. John Wesley (Col.)
Freeman, 2d Lt. Edward T. (1st Lt.)
Frost, 2d Lt. George H. (Capt.)

Gainslin, Asst. Surg. J. J.
Gallimard, Capt. Jules Victor
Galt, 2d Lt. J. Allan (Capt.)
Galt, Capt. John M. (Maj.)
Gamble, 2d Lt. Lewis M.
Garden, 2d Lt. Henry DeSaussure (Capt.)
Gardner, Lt. Col. Franklin (Maj. Gen.)
Gardner, Maj. William Montgomery
  (Brig. Gen.)
Garland, Capt. Robert R. (Col.)
Garner, 1st Lt. George G. (Lt. Col.)
Garnett, 2d Lt. James M. (Capt.)
Garnett, 2d Lt. John J. (Lt. Col.)

Garnett, Maj. Richard Brooke
  (Brig. Gen.)*
Garnett, Lt. Col. Robert S. (Brig. Gen.)*
Garrard, Cadet Louis F.
Gatlin, Col. Richard Caswell (Brig. Gen.)
Gayle, 1st Lt. Matt
Getty, 1st Lt. G. Thomas (Capt.)
Gibbes, 1st Lt. Wade H. (Maj.)
Gibbon, Capt. Lardner
Gibbs, Capt. George C. (Col.)
Gibson, 2d Lt. William E. (Capt.)
Gill, Capt. William G. (Col.)
Gillispie, Cadet George L.
Gilmer, Col. Jeremy Francis (Maj. Gen.)
Godwin, 1st Lt. Archibald Campbell
  (Brig. Gen.)*
Goode, 2d Lt. Edward B. (1st Lt.)
Goode, Capt. John Thomas (Col.)
Gorgas, Lt. Col. Josiah (Brig. Gen.)
Graham, 2d Lt. Charles M. (Capt.)
Grant, 2d Lt. Robert (Capt.)
Grasty, Cadet Samuel J.
Gray, Capt. A. B.*
Grayson, 2d Lt. Thomas T.
Griffin, Cadet Andrew
Griffith, 2d Lt. Richard Cephas
Groner, 1st Lt. Virginius D. (Col.)
Guild, Surg. LaFayette

Haden, Surg. John M.
Hagood, 2d Lt. J.
Hairston, 2d Lt. J. T. Watt (Maj.)
Haley, 2d Lt. Alfred G. (1st Lt.)
Hall, Cadet R. B.
Hallam, Cadet T. F.
Hallonquist, 1st Lt. James H. (Lt. Col.)
Hamilton, 2d Lt. James (Maj.)
Hammett, Cadet M. A.
Hanson, Cadet Isaac N.
Hardcastle, Capt. Aaron B. (Col.)
Hardee, Col. William Joseph (Lt. Gen.)
Harlee, Cadet E. P.
Harris, Cadet James E.
Harris, 2d Lt. W. A.
Harris, 2d Lt. W. H.
Harrison, Cadet Thomas
Hartley, 2d Lt. A. J. (Capt.)
Harvie, Capt. Edward James (Col.)

Haskell, 1st Lt. Alexander M. (Maj.)
Haskell, Cadet James Cheeves
Hatcher, Cadet J. W. D.
Hawes, Capt. James Morrison (Brig. Gen.)
Hayne, 2d Lt. Theodore B. (Capt.)
Helm, 1st Lt. Benjamin Hardin (Brig. Gen.)*
Helm, 2d Lt. Charles J.
Henry, 2d Lt. Gustavus A., Jr. (Lt. Col.)
Henry, 2d Lt. Mathias Winston (Maj.)
Herbert, 1st Lt. Waters W. (Maj.)
Herndon, Asst. Surg. James C.
Heth, Maj. Henry (Maj. Gen.)
Heywood, 2d Lt. Duncan C.
Hill, 2d Lt. Charles S. (Capt.)
Hill, 1st Lt. Gabriel H. (Lt. Col.)
Hill, 1st Lt. James H. (Maj.)
Hill, 1st Lt. Robert C. (Col.)
Hill, 2d Lt. William E. (Capt.)
Holman, 1st Lt. James H. (Col.)
Holmes, Col. Theophilus H. (Lt. Gen.)
Holmes, Cadet Theophilus H., Jr.*
Holt, 1st Lt. George W. (Maj.)
Hood, Capt. John Bell (Gen.)
Hooe, 2d Lt. Roy Mason (Capt.)
Hooper, 2d Lt. Charles M. (1st Lt.)
Hooper, 2d Lt. William DeBerniere
Hopkins, Cadet James E. M.
House, Cadet John M.
Houston, Cadet John W.
Howard, 1st Lt. James (Lt. Col.)
Howell, Capt. William F.
Hoxton, 1st Lt. Llewellyn G. (Lt. Col.)
Huger, Col. Benjamin (Maj. Gen.)
Huger, 1st Lt. Benjamin, Jr. (Capt.)
Huger, 2d Lt. Frank (Col.)
Hullihen, 2d Lt. Walter Q. (Capt.)
Humphreys, Capt. Frederick Clinton (Maj.)
Humphries, 2d Lt. William D. (Capt.)
Hunt, 2d Lt. Thomas W. (Capt.)
Hunter, Cadet H. W.
Hunter, 2d Lt. James, Jr.
Hunter, Cadet James D. (2d Lt.)
Huse, Capt. Caleb (Maj.)
Hutchins, Cadet Clarence L.
Hutter, 2d Lt. Edward S. (Maj.)
Hyams, Cadet E. L.
Hyams, 2d Lt. Isaac S. (Capt.)

Ingraham, 1st Lt. Edward (Maj.)*
Ingraham, 1st Lt. H. Laurens (Capt.)
Iverson, Capt. Alfred (Brig. Gen.)
Ives, Capt. Jospeh Christmas (Col.)

Jackson, 1st Lt. Andrew, Jr. (Col.)
Jackson, 2d Lt. Columbus L. (Capt.)
Jackson, 1st Lt. George (Col.)
Jackson, Cadet Henry
Jackson, Maj. Thomas Jonathan
　(Lt. Gen.)*
Jackson, Capt. Thomas Klugh (Maj.)
Jackson, 1st Lt. William Hicks (Brig. Gen.)
James, Capt. George S. (Lt. Col.)*
Johns, Cadet Edward W.
Johns, 1st Lt. John
Johnson, Cadet B. S. (Maj.)
Johnson, Lt. Col. Edward (Maj. Gen.)
Johnson, Cadet Madison C.
Johnson, Cadet Peyton L.
Johnston, Gen. Albert Sidney*
Johnston, Gen. Joseph Eggleston
Johnston, 2d Lt. Joseph Forney (1st Lt.)
Jones, Maj. David Rumph (Maj. Gen.)
Jones, 2d Lt. Frank F. (Maj.)
Jones, Maj. John Marshall (Brig. Gen.)*
Jones, 1st Lt. Joseph Peck (Col.)
Jones, Cadet M. H.
Jones, Maj. Samuel (Maj. Gen.)
Jones, Capt. Thomas Marshall (Col.)
Jones, Capt. Walter (Maj.)
Jones, 2d Lt. William R. (Capt.)
Jordan, Capt. Thomas (Brig. Gen.)

Kearny, 1st Lt. William (Maj.)
Keeble, 2d Lt. James M. (1st Lt.)
Keith, 2d Lt. John A. (1st Lt.)
Kelly, Capt. Henry Brooke (Col.)
Kelly, 2d Lt. John Herbert (Brig. Gen.)*
Kennard, 1st Lt. James M. (Lt. Col.)
Kenner, 2d Lt. Minor, Jr.
Ker, 2d Lt. James (Capt.)
Kerr, 2d Lt. Severn P. (1st Lt.)
Keyworth, 2d Lt. Robert W. (Maj.)
Kimmel, 2d Lt. Manning M. (Maj.)
King, Capt. A. W.
King, 2d Lt. Benjamin*
King, Cadet C. A.
King, 1st Lt. H. Lord P. (Capt.)*

Kinney, 2d Lt. Richard Stevenson (Capt.)
Kirby, 2d Lt. Joseph Lee Smith (Capt.)
Kirkland, Capt. William Whedbee
  (Brig. Gen.)
Knox, Cadet Robert H.
Knox, 1st Lt. William

Lamar, Cadet G. D.
Lamar, Cadet William T.
Lambert, 1st Lt. Richard (Capt.)
Landworth, Surg. E. P.
Lane, 2d Lt. John (Lt. Col.)
Lanier, 2d Lt. John S.
Law, 1st Lt. Junius (Lt. Col.)
Lawton, 1st Lt. Edward P. (Capt.)*
Lay, Capt. George William (Lt. Col.)
Lea, 2d Lt. John W. (Lt. Col.)
Leadbetter, Maj. Danville (Brig. Gen.)
Lee, 1st Lt. Charles C. (Col.)*
Lee, 1st Lt. Fitzhugh (Maj. Gen.)
Lee, Capt. George Washington Custis
  (Maj. Gen.)
Lee, 2d Lt. John M. (Maj.)
Lee, Lt. Col. Richard Bland
Lee, Gen. Robert Edward
Lee, Cadet Robert Edward, Jr. (Capt.)
Lee, Capt. Stephen Dill (Lt. Gen.)
Lee, 1st Lt. W. F.
Legare, 1st Lt. John J. (Capt.)
Lewis, Cadet John
Lewis, Capt. Theodore
Lewis, Cadet William (2d Lt.)
Lindsay, Maj. Andrew Jackson (Col.)
Lindsay, 2d Lt. Mott M. (1st Lt.)
Lipscomb, 2d Lt. James N. (Capt.)
Little, Maj. Lewis Henry (Brig. Gen.)*
Lockett, Capt. Samuel Henry (Col.)
Logan, 2d Lt. Robert H. (Lt. Col.)
Lomax, 1st Lt. Lunsford Lindsay
  (Maj. Gen.)
Long, Capt. Armistead Lindsay
  (Brig. Gen.)
Long, 1st Lt. John Osmond (Lt. Col.)
Longstreet, Lt. Col. James (Lt. Gen.)
Loring, Col. William Wing (Maj. Gen.)
Lovejoy, 2d Lt. George S. (Lt. Col.)
Lucas, 2d Lt. Alfred P.
Lumpkin, 2d Lt. Charles M.

Lyon, 1st Lt. Hylan Benton (Brig. Gen.)
Lyon, 2d Lt. William Dunn (Capt.)

Mackall, Lt. Col. William Whann
  (Brig. Gen.)
Maclin, 2d Lt. Thomas
Madison, Surg. Thomas C.
Magruder, Cadet George A., Jr. (Maj.)
Magruder, Col. John Bankhead
  (Maj. Gen.)
Major, 1st Lt. James Patrick (Brig. Gen.)
Mallory, 1st Lt. Francis (Col.)*
Manning, 2d Lt. Peyton T. (Lt. Col.)
Marchbanks, 2d Lt. George
Marshall, Cadet H., Jr.
Martin, Capt. James Green (Brig. Gen.)
Masi, Cadet Frank J.
Mason, 2d Lt. James M., Jr. (Capt.)
Massie, 2d Lt. John L. (Capt.)*
Maury, Capt. Dabney Herndon
  (Maj. Gen.)
Maxwell, Cadet Simeon
Mayes, 2d Lt. Joseph D. (1st Lt.)
Mayo, 1st Lt. George U. (Maj.)
McCall, 1st Lt. James K. (Maj.)
McConnell, Capt. Thomas Rush
McCown, Lt. Col. John Porter
  (Maj. Gen.)
McCreery, 1st Lt. William Westwood
  (Capt.)*
McDonald, 2d Lt. C. Wood*
McDonald, 2d Lt. Marshall (Capt.)
McFarland, 1st Lt. James Davis (Capt.)
McIntosh, Capt. James McQueen
  (Brig. Gen.)*
McIntosh, 2d Lt. Thomas Spalding (Maj.)*
McIver, Cadet Evander
McLaws, Maj. Lafayette (Maj. Gen.)
McLean, Lt. Col. Eugene Eckel
McLemore, 1st Lt. Owen Kenan (Lt. Col.)*
McMain, 1st Lt. William H. (Capt.)
McNab, Cadet John M.
McNeill, 1st Lt. Henry C. (Col.)
Meade, 2d Lt. Richard K. (1st Lt.)
Meade, 1st Lt. Richard Kidder, Jr. (Maj.)
Mercer, 1st Lt. John Thomas (Col.)*
Mercer, Cadet Thomas H. (2d Lt.)
Merchant, Capt. Anderson (Lt. Col.)

Miller, Cadet E. Van Dorn
Miller, Cadet Pinckney Orr
Minter, Maj. Joseph F.
Mitchell, Cadet Charles E.
Mohler, 2d Lt. E. G. (Maj.)
Montgomery, 1st Lt. Alexander B. (Col.)
Moore, 2d Lt. Alexander D. (Col.)*
Moore, Capt. John Creed (Brig. Gen.)
Moore, Cadet Rittenhouse
Moore, Col. Samuel Preston
Moreno, 2d Lt. Stephen A. (Capt.)
Moreno, 1st Lt. Theodore (Capt.)
Morgan, 2nd Lt. Charles S. (Capt.)
Morgan, Cadet E. F.
Morgan, 2d Lt. William Henry (Capt.)*
Morrison, Capt. R. J.
Morton, Cadet S. D.
Mouton, Capt. Jean Jacques Alfred
  Alexander (Big Gen.)*
Myers, Col. Abraham Charles

Napier, 1st Lt. Leroy, Jr. (Lt. Col.)
Nelson, 2d Lt. Richard M. (Capt.)
Niemeyer, 2d Lt. William F. (Lt. Col.)*
Northrop, Col. Lucius Ballinger

O'Bannon, Maj. Laurence W. (Lt. Col.)
Obenchain, 2d Lt. William A. (Capt.)
O'Brien, 2d Lt. John F. (Maj.)
Ochiltree, 2d Lt. William B. Jr. (1st Lt.)
O'Hara, Capt. Theodore (Lt. Col.)
Oladowaski, Capt. Hypolite (Lt. Col.)
Olivier, Cadet Leonce N.
O'Neal, 2d Lt. Alfred M. (Capt.)
O'Neal, Cadet Edward A., Jr.
Orton, 1st Lt. Lawrence William (Col.)*
Otey, 1st Lt. George Gaston (Capt.)
Overton, 1st Lt. Thomas (Capt.)

Page, Cadet Philip Nelson
Palfrey, Maj. Edward Augustus
Parker, 2d Lt. James P. (Lt. Col.)
Parker, Cadet S. H., Jr.
Patterson, 1st Lt. Charles E. (Lt. Col.)*
Payne, 2d Lt. John D.
Peck, 1st Lt. Lafayette
Pelham, 1st Lt. John (Lt. Col.)*
Pemberton, Lt. Col. John Clifford
  (Lt. Gen.)

Pender, Capt. William Dorsey
  (Maj. Gen.)*
Pendleton, Capt. William Nelson
  (Brig. Gen.)
Perkins, 2d Lt. Frederick H. (1st Lt.)
Phifer, 1st Lt. Charles W. (Lt. Col.)
Phillips, 2d Lt. Joseph (Col.)*
Phillips, Capt. T. Moses
Pickens, 2d Lt. Samuel B. (Col.)
Pickett, Maj. George Edward (Maj. Gen.)
Polignac, Lt. Col. Camille Armand Jules
  Marie de (Maj. Gen.)
Poor, 2d Lt. R. L. (Maj.)
Porcher, Cadet C. P.
Porter, 1st Lt. William C.
Porter, 2d Lt. William H. (1st Lt.)
Porter, Cadet William H.
Portlock, 2d Lt. E. E., Jr. (Col.)
Potts, Surg. Richard
Powell, 2d Lt. Edward (Maj.)
Powell, Capt. William L.
Price, Capt. Thomas J.

Quattlebaum, 1st Lt. Paul Jones (Lt. Col.)

Raines, Cadet W. A. (Capt.)
Rains, Col. Gabriel James (Brig. Gen.)
Ramseur, Asst. Surg. David P.
Ramseur, 1st Lt. Stephen Dodson
  (Maj. Gen.)*
Randal, 1st Lt. Horace (Brig. Gen.)*
Randolph, 1st Lt. Peyton (Maj.)
Ranson, 2d Lt. Ambrose R. H. (Maj.)
Rea, Capt. Constantine (Maj.)*
Reedy, Cadet James H.
Reid, Cadet Joseph Davis*
Revely, 2d Lt. W. W. (1st Lt.)
Reynolds, Capt. Alexander Welch
  (Brig. Gen.)
Reynolds, 2d Lt. Frank A. (Lt. Col.)
Reynolds, 2d Lt. George N. (Maj.)
Reynolds, Capt. Samuel H. (Maj.)
Rhett, 1st Lt. Alfred (Col.)
Rhett, Capt. Thomas Smith (Col.)
Rice, 2d Lt. Olin F. (Col.)
Rice, 2d Lt. Samuel F., Jr.
Rich, Capt. Lucius Loomis (Col.)*
Richardson, 2d Lt. Charles (Lt. Col.)
Richmond, 1st Lt. William B.*

Riddick, 1st Lt. Richard H. (Col.)*
Riley, 2d Lt. Edward Bishop Dudley
    (Capt.)
Ringo, Cadet Daniel W.*
Roberts, Capt. William W.
Robertson, 2d Lt. Felix Huston
    (Brig. Gen.)
Robertson, Capt. Beverly Holcombe
    (Brig. Gen.)
Robinson, 2d Lt. William George (Col.)
Ross, 2d Lt. Edward M.
Ross, 2d Lt. Ebenezer McEwen
Rosser, 1st Lt. Thomas Lafayette
    (Maj. Gen.)
Rowland, 1st Lt. Alexander M. (Maj.)
Rowland, Cadet Thomas
Rucker, 1st Lt. Edmund Winchester (Col.)
Rudd, 2d Lt. John Speed
Ruggles, Col. Daniel (Brig. Gen.)
Russell, 2d Lt. J. B. (Capt.)
Rutledge, 2d Lt. Henry (Col)
Ryals, 2d Lt. Garland M. (Maj.)

St. Clair, 2d Lt. George B. (1st Lt.)
Sandidge, 2d Lt. Lucius D. (Capt.)
Saunders, 1st Lt. John Seldon (Lt. Col.)
Shaeffer, 2d Lt. Francis B. (Maj.)
Scott, Capt. John (Maj.)
Scriven, 2d Lt. Richard D.
Sergeant, Cadet Thomas
Selden, 1st Lt. William B.*
Selph, 2d Lt. Colin McRae (Capt.)
Semmes, 2d Lt. Oliver J. (Maj.)
Semple, 2d Lt. Edward A. (Capt.)
Schaaff, 1st Lt. Arthur (Maj.)
Schaaff, Capt. John Thomas
Selden, 1st Lt. William B.*
Shields, 2d Lt. E. B.*
Shoup, 1st Lt. Francis Asbury (Brig. Gen.)
Sibley, Lt. Col. Henry Hopkins
    (Brig. Gen.)
Simpson, Cadet J. N.
Skinner, Cadet Thomas
Slaughter, Capt. James Edwin (Brig. Gen.)
Sloan, 1st Lt. Benjamin F., Jr. (Maj.)
Smead, 1st Lt. Abner (Col.)
Smith, Capt. Caleb (Maj.)
Smith, Surg. Charles Henry

Smith, Lt. Col. Edmund Kirby (Gen.)
Smith, Cadet F. W.
Smith, 2d Lt. George Hampton (Lt. Col.)
Smith, Capt. James Argyle (Brig. Gen.)
Smith, 2d Lt. John N.
Smith, Lt. Col. Larkin (Col.)
Smith, 2d Lt. L. Jaquelin (Capt.)
Smith, Maj. Martin Luther (Maj. Gen.)
Smith, 1st Lt. Richard Inge
Smith, Capt. William Duncan (Brig. Gen.)
Smith, Capt. William Proctor (Col.)
Smith, Capt. W. N.
Snead, 1st Lt. Thomas T. L. (Capt.)
Snowden, 2d Lt. John Hudson
Sorrel, Surg. Francis
Sparks, 2d Lt. Jesse W. (1st Lt.)
Spence, 2d Lt. Philip B. (Lt. Col.)
Stafford, Cadet Fred M. (2d Lt.)
Stafford, Cadet John C.
Stansbury, Capt. Smith (Lt. Col.)
Stark, Cadet E. B.
Starr, Cadet James F.
Steen, Capt. Alexander Early (Brig. Gen.)*
Steuart, Capt. George Hume (Brig. Gen.)
Stevens, Maj. Walter Husted (Brig. Gen.)
Stevenson, Lt. Col. Carter Littlepage
    (Maj. Gen.)
Stewart, 2d Lt. Joseph Henry
Stith, Capt. Donald Chester (Col.)
Stockton, Capt. Philip (Col.)
Stockton, Capt. William Telfair (Lt. Col.)
Stone, Cadet Marshall N.
Stoney, 2d Lt. William E. (Capt.)
Storrs, 1st Lt. George Strong (Maj.)
Summers, Cadet John T.
Sweetman, 2d Lt. Robert L. (Capt.)
Sykes, 2d Lt. Eugene Octavius (Capt.)
Sykes, Cadet James P. (2d Lt.)

Tabb, 2d Lt. William Kemp (Capt.)
Talcott, 1st Lt. Thomas M. R. (Col.)
Taliaferro, 1st Lt. Edwin (Maj.)
Taliaferro, 2d Lt. John
Talley, 2d Lt. Robert A.
Tansill, Capt. Robert (Col.)
Taylor, 1st Lt. Edmund
Taylor, 1st Lt. John Gibson (Lt. Col.)*
Taylor, Capt. Thomas Hary (Col.)

Taylor, 1st Lt. Walter Herron (Lt. Col.)
Taylor, 2d Lt. William V. (Maj.)
Terrett, Cadet Burdett A. (Capt.)
Thomas, 1st Lt. Bryan Morel (Brig. Gen.)
Thomas, 1st Lt. Robert Brenham (Col.)
Thompson, Cadet John B.
Thompson, Cadet W. W.*
Thornton, 2d Lt. George A. (Capt.)
Todd, 1st Lt. David H. (Capt.)*
Todd, Cadet James
Tracy, 2d Lt. Campbell (Capt.)
Tranun, 2d Lt. William T.
Truehart, 1st Lt. Daniel (Maj.)
Tucker, Cadet S. M.
Turner, 2d Lt. Thomas Pratt (Maj.)
Turpin, 2d Lt. Walter G. (Capt.)
Twyman, 2d Lt. Horace D. (Capt.)
Tyler, Capt. Charles Humphrey (Col.)
Tyler, 2d Lt. William (Capt.)

Van Dorn, Col. Earl (Maj. Gen.)
Venable, 1st Lt. Charles S. (Lt. Col.)
Villepique, Capt. John Bordenave.
  (Brig. Gen.)

Waddy, 1st Lt. John Robinson (Lt. Col.)
Wade, Cadet E. Barksdale
Wagner, Capt. Charles G. (Maj.)
Walker, 2d Lt. C. Irvine (Lt. Col.)
Walker, Capt. Henry Harrison (Brig. Gen.)
Walker, Capt. John D. (Maj.)*
Walker, Maj. John George (Maj. Gen.)
Walker, 2d Lt. John P. (Capt.)
Walker, Capt. William Stephen
  (Brig. Gen.)
Wall, Asst. Surg. Asa
Waller, Cadet W. G.
Walton, Cadet John M.
Wankowicz, 2d Lt. Ladislas (Capt.)
Warley, 2d Lt. J. Hamilton (Capt.)
Washburn, 2d Lt. Henry K. (Capt.)
Washington, 2d Lt. James Barroll (1st Lt.)
Washington, 2d Lt. James E. McPherson
Washington, Maj. Thornton Augustine
Watie, Cadet Saladin
Watkins, 2d Lt. Anderson (Lt. Col.)*
Watts, 2d Lt. George Owen (Maj.)
Watts, Capt. N. G. (Col.)

Weatherly, Cadet Colin M. R.
Webster, 2d Lt. William Eugene (1st Lt.)*
Welcker, Capt. William Thomas
West, 2d Lt. John Asbury A. (Maj.)
Wheeler, 1st Lt. Joseph (Maj. Gen.)
White, 2d Lt. Benjamin S. (Maj.)
White, 2d Lt. David G. (Col.)
White, Capt. James Lyon (Lt. Col.)
White, 1st Lt. Moses James (Lt. Col.)
White, 1st Lt. Oscar (Lt. Col.)
Whiting, Capt. Jasper S.
Whiting, Maj. William Henry Chase
  (Maj. Gen.)*
Wickliffe, 1st Lt. Nathaniel (Lt. Col.)
Wigfall, Cadet Francis H. (Maj.)
Wilcox, Capt. Cadmus Marcellus
  (Maj. Gen.)
Wilkins, 2d Lt. Hamilton
Wilkinson, 2d Lt. Willis (Capt.)
Willett, 2d Lt. Zadock T. (Capt.)*
Williams, 1st Lt. Samuel C. (Lt. Col.)
Williams, 1st Lt. Soloman (Col.)*
Williams, Maj. Thomas Greenhow
  (Lt. Col.)
Williams, Surg. Thomas H.
Willis, 2d Lt. Edward S. (Col.)*
Willson, 2d Lt. Tom Friend (Capt.)
Winchester, Cadet N. B.
Winder, Maj. Charles Sidney (Brig. Gen.)*
Winder, Col. John Henry (Brig. Gen.)
Winston, Col. Cadet W. O.
Wintersmith, Cadet James G.
Wise, 2d Lt. George D. (Capt.)*
Withers, Maj. John (Lt. Col.)
Withers, 2d Lt. William F.
Wood, Capt. Robert Crooke, Jr. (Lt. Col.)
Woodson, Cadet William
Worthington, 2d Lt. Winfield C.
Wright, 1st Lt. Moses H. (Col.)

Yancy, Capt. Benjamin C., Jr. (Lt. Col.)
Yancey, Cadet Thomas B.
Yates, 1st Lt. Joseph A. (Lt. Col.)
Young, 2d Lt. Pierce Manning Butler
  (Maj. Gen.)

Zacharie, 1st Lt. Francis C. (Col.)
Zulasky, 2d Lt. Sigismund (1st Lt.)

Appendix B

ORGANIZATION OF THE CONFEDERATE REGULAR ARMY

	GENERALS	A.A.G. — COLONEL	A.A.G. — LT. COL.	A.A.G. — MAJORS	A.A.G. — CAPTAINS	Q.M.G. — COLONEL	A.Q.M.G. — LT. COL.	A.Q.M. — MAJORS	COM. GENL. — COLONEL	COMMISSARY — LT. COL.	COMMISSARY — MAJORS	COMMISSARY — CAPTAINS	SURG. GENL. — COLONEL	SURGEONS — MAJORS	ASST. SURGEONS	COLONELS	LIEUTENANT COLONELS	MAJORS	CAPTAINS
General Officers	5																		
ADC to General Officer																			
Adjutant General Dept.		1	2	2	4											1			
Quartermaster General Dept.						1	2	6	1	1	2	4							
Commissary General Dept.									1	1	2	4							
Medical Department													1	10	21				
Corps of Engineers																1	1	4	10
Co. of Sappers & Bombardiers																			1
Corps of Artillery																1	2	12	40
Two Regiments of Cavalry																2	2	2	20
Eight Regiments of Infantry																8	8	8	80
Regiment of Zouaves																1	1	1	10
Total	5	1	2	2	4	1	2	6	1	1	2	4	1	10	21	13	14	27	161

a. The 10 Aide-de-camps being taken from the lieutenants of the line, in the strength of which they are included, to avoid counting them twice they are excluded as staff officers in the columns of total commissioned and aggregate. The Adjutants, being selected from the regiments of infantry and cavalry and the Corps of Artillery, are excluded as above.

b. Sergeants major being selected from the enlisted men, to avoid being counted twice are excluded from the total enlisted and aggregate. Hospital stewards and ordnance sergeants are not included in the above, the number of the former being determined by the Secretary of War and the latter by the number of military posts.

ADJUTANTS	1ST LIEUTENANTS	2D LIEUTENANTS	SUPT. OF ARMORY	MASTER ARMORERS	M.S.K. OF ORD. – CAPT.	M.S.K. – 1ST LT.	SERGEANTS MAJOR	QUARTERMASTER SERGEANTS	ORDNANCE SERGEANTS	SERGEANTS	CORPORALS	MUSICIANS	FARRIERS & BLACKSMITHS	ARTIFICERS	PRIVATES	ENLISTED MEN OF ORDNANCE	TOTAL COMMISSIONED	TOTAL ENLISTED	AGGREGATE
																	5		5
																	9		9
																	9		9
																	8		8
																	32		32
										10	10	2		39	39		16	100	116
	2	1								10	10	2		39	39		4	100	104
1[a]	80	40	1[c]	2	4	6	1[b]			200	160	80			2,800	100	188	3,460	3,648
2[a]	20	40					2[b]	2	2	100	80	40	40		1,200		86	1,462	1,550
8[a]	80	160					8[b]	8	8	400	320	160			7,200		344	8,088	8,440
1[a]	10	20						1	10	50	80				900		43	1,050	1,094
12	192	261	1	2	4	6	11	20	10[b]	770	660	284	40	78	12,178	100	744	14,260	15,015

c. Or more.

d. Cadets are not enumerated as the President was to appoint them from the several states in number proportionate to the Representatives in the House of Representatives and 10 at large.

Index